123

Frisky Sexual Fantasies

&

Erotic Roleplay Ideas

Dare to Play Naughty
Sexy Scenarios for Couples

Michael and Barbara Kortekaas

Succulent Enterprises Inc.

Copyright © 2013 Michael & Barbara Kortekaas

Cover Image: Fotolia

Cover Design: Michael Kortekaas

Dedication

This book is dedicated to all couples striving to create a loving, long lasting relationship that is filled with joy and happiness. We hope this book inspires you to creatively enhance your relationship with even more fun and pleasure. Stay frisky and playful as you grow even closer together.

Play Safe

Succulent Enterprises Inc. and the authors assume no responsibility for any injury or damage incurred while playing or performing any activities inspired or identified in this book. The fantasy roleplay ideas are intended for consenting adults who are knowledgeable of sex while still exploring and discovering their full sexual potential. If you have any health concerns, please consult your doctor to ensure you're healthy and fit enough to engage in sex.

Sex is a very sensitive subject. People have radically different views on what is morally right and wrong when it comes to sex between consenting adults. Although attitudes have become more accepting of a broader range of sexual practices, many laws still exist that prohibit specific types of sexual activities. Certain sections of this book may deal with activities that could be in violation of various federal, state and local laws if actually carried out in your location. We do not advocate breaking any law. The authors and publisher do not accept liability for any injury, loss, legal consequence, or incidental or consequential damage incurred by reliance on information, advice or suggestions provided in this book. The information in this book is for entertainment purposes only.

Always use safer sex practices and common sense when performing or engaging in any sexual activity. Sample activities provided are designed for couples in a monogamous sexual relationship. All the foreplay and sex play ideas are intended to inspire your own sexual creativity so you can enhance your relationship with more pleasure and intimacy. They are only sexy suggestions for you to adapt and perform at your own discretion.

Special Note: always clean before inter-mixing anal then vaginal activities to avoid bacterial infections. Also avoid getting anything with sugar in the vagina. This can lead to a nasty yeast infection.

Dare Your Lover to Play Naughty

With You Tonight

Introduction

Welcome to our collection of **123 Frisky Sexual Fantasies & Erotic Roleplay Ideas**. This book is intended for couples who want to make their sex life even more fun. We've included a broad range of sexy scenarios to suit a variety of interests and desires. Each idea is designed to stimulate your erotic imagination and enhance your sexual creativity. We hope they get you fantasizing and talking about ways to bring them to life in and out of your bedroom. To spice up your intimate times together, pick an idea and dare each other to play naughty.

The scenarios in this book are more than just a list of simplistic roles like "Teacher and Student". We wanted to provide you with a plausible reason why each of the various characters are in the situation that leads to sex. Certain aspects of the character's personality and motivations are also identified so you know basically how they're expected to behave and react to each other. This way you and your partner will be on the same page when thinking about how the scene will play out. There's nothing worse then roleplaying a student expecting to be punished by the teacher for being bad while the teacher is expecting to be seduced and offered sex for improved grades. Neither one of your desires will be satisfied.

Also, rather than having an extensive storyline and dialogue that you need to memorize, we created role descriptions with just enough detail to quickly set the stage and get the action started. By not completely specifying the scripts, you are more free to improvise and adjust them to include your own sexual preferences. There is just enough information to stimulate your imagination, get you talking about alternate possibilities and enable you to weave in elements of your own fantasies. You can even replay the scenarios multiple times to try out new activities. You're bound to come up with completely new tantalizing twists and turn ons every time.

We also wanted to provide a large variety of roleplay ideas that encourage you to use sex toys and other erotic accessories together. It's a shame to have a drawer full of pleasure enhancing products that never seem to get used as often as you'd like. It's even more of a shame if you haven't had a good excuse to try any yet. In this book, you'll find that some scenarios set up the context where using toys or other kinky devices seems more appropriate than when you're just having "regular" sex. For example, bondage play can be more fun when there's a reason for one of you to be tied up. Also, dildos and vibrators come in handy as special props for some of the scenarios. What ever intimate items you have available, you're sure to find a scenario in which to creatively use them.

The scenarios are grouped into sections based on a common theme or type of encounter. The section title gives a fairly strong hint as to the types of fantasy situations available in the group but there is a lot of variation between each of the scenarios. There is a brief introduction for each section that highlights the common elements, provides additional roleplay details and outlines ideas to make the scene more realistic. Each scenario is given a suggestive title and a number from 1 to 123. These titles are a little more cryptic as to what's actually involved in order to arouse your curiosity. Each scenario gives a brief story outline and a list of optional suggestions including sample lines of dialogue, potential props, types of dress, etc.

There are a number of ways you can play with the sexy scenarios in this book. Although written as roleplay ideas, they are perfect for starting a sexy conversation to explore each other's erotic fantasies and sexual desires. You can pick one and challenge each other to come up with the best dirty story involving the two of you. Make up the sexy details and climax to the story before, during or after sex. If you're apart, keep the passion on simmer by telling each other a dirty story over the phone, via web camera, text messaging, through email or even handwritten for that personal touch. And of course you can also use ideas in this book to fuel your own private fantasies.

You can go through each scenario in sequence to try them all or choose a way to randomly select one and make it a sexy surprise for both of you. You can even make the scenario selection part of any game you enjoy playing. Use the score in some way to determine the number of a scenario. Or you can let your partner choose a section title while you choose one of the scenarios in that group just based on the title alone (no peeking). Any way you decide to play with these frisky sexual scenarios, we hope you create special and memorable moments together that are loving and fun. Enjoy your adult playtime as often as you can.

Sharing Sexual Fantasies

Great sex becomes amazing sex when your mind is turned on just as much as your body. Whether alone masturbating or having sex with a partner, you can close your eyes and let a steamy fantasy push you to ever higher levels of delicious ecstasy. In just a few moments you can transport yourself into a new sexual situation that is exciting and arousing. There are so many erotic possibilities to enjoy. The variety of wild sexual adventures you can experience is limitless. With sexual fantasies you can be anyone and do anyone any where any time. You can indulge all your deepest darkest desires with no guilt, shame or danger. And best of all, your imagination is free.

A fantasy can be as simple as pretending to be in a different place or making love to a different person. Even thinking how you want to make love with your partner later is fantasizing. Recalling past lovemaking experiences is also fantasizing. It doesn't even have to be very explicit or visual – just recalling a feeling or sensation can get you in the mood for more. Fantasies can also be complex and elaborate with entire stories wrapped around the various events leading to an ultimate sexual climax. They may involve detailed characters, settings and situations combined with specific objects or words with deep emotional triggers that get you extra hot.

Sexual fantasy can even help couples in a committed relationship resist the temptation to cheat. If you're in a long term relationship, your sex life may be getting a little dull, routine or even a tad boring at times. Many people end up having an affair to satisfy their own sexual needs that could easily be fulfilled in their relationship. Many times the need is just for more sexual variety which could be easily addressed with shared or private fantasies. We all need to feel the excitement of doing something new and out of the ordinary but it doesn't have to involve sex with other people.

Novelty is a crucial ingredient for keeping your passion for each other energized. You may already be using private fantasies to make sex more exciting. And if you're not, it's a perfect time to start. Either way, consider revealing some of your erotic thoughts to your partner so they can share in your excitement. Discussing sex together will encourage you both to try out new things with each other rather than just keeping it private or worse, sharing them with someone else. Many people fear that their partner will reject their ideas or think they're a pervert or slut. Sharing fantasies is a delicate act that takes courage especially in an intimate, caring, stable and comfortable relationship.

Although there are emotional risks involved, you can dramatically enhance, improve and possibly even save your relationship and your sex life by sharing fantasies with your lover. That's where the ideas in this book come into play. Each scenario has been written to set the stage for a sexual encounter without specifying all the details of what's going to happen. Also, the basic character roles are indicated but how they behave and how they perform various activities is left to your imagination. Just choose a scenario in the book and challenge each other to fill in more and more of the details verbally. Each of you just need to describe a little bit more of the action to lead the story forward and then alternate. The key is to make it a game competing with each other to creatively crank up the erotic heat a few more degrees each round. Like foreplay, you want to start off relatively slow and increase the intensity gradually. As you become more comfortable building onto your combined story, have the characters engage in some kinkier activities. As fantasy directors, have the characters in your story indulge in a variety of wickedly deviant pleasures and observe how your partner responds. When the opportunity seems right, weave in hints of your secret desires and see where they lead. Since the objective is to come up with the wildest and most sexually explicit story you can, your true desires can be mixed into the action without feeling inhibited.

As you gain confidence expressing more details of your secret sexual desires in these steamy story sessions, you'll naturally feel more comfortable talking more openly about what you want and enjoy. It will take a few times with different starting scenarios to really get the hang of it. But, in the process you'll discover new ways to pleasure each other and practice talking dirty together. You can also enjoy this type of dirty story creation in writing if you prefer. Each of you would write a paragraph before exchanging it with your partner to continue where you left off. You could do this on paper, by email or even texting. Any way you do it, you're bound to have lots of frisky fun together mentally experimenting with all sorts of potential sexual experiences.

By involving each other in this creative erotic adventure, you can spice up your desire for each other leading to more passionate and fulfilling sex. It gives you the opportunity to share what turns you on. Although it's rare that you'll both get the same thrill from any one particular fantasy, sharing your fantasies can lead you toward a greater level of trust and empathy for each other. And, as you continue to creatively explore your erotic imaginations together, you're bound to discover many thrilling fantasies that satisfy both your desires. It's also great practice for eventually roleplaying together and bringing your fantasies to life.

Starting to Roleplay

When you first start to add roleplaying to your bedroom games, it can feel a little awkward and uncomfortable. Unless you're a born actor, getting your mind to think and behave like a different character is challenging at first. As discussed in the section on sharing fantasies, you can get used to the roles by describing the story and talking dirty with each other while making love. In fact, it's best to try out a roleplay scenario in this way before investing in any costumes, special accessories or props.

Some character roles will feel more familiar based on past experiences (books read, movies seen, personal encounters, etc.). For others, you may find it useful to do some research to discover more details about the characters and setting. It may even be helpful to give your character a name that you can identify with. Also, make up a fake past with as much detail as you can to feel more connected with the role. If you can locate a movie with related characters or scenes, consider watching it together so you can both pick up more ideas to include in your erotic version. You might find an appealing accent or certain behaviours that you can imitate.

Although special outfits and accessories are optional, sometimes they do help you get into character easier. Of course, certain types of uniforms or styles of dress are just plain sexy. The erotic appeal of some scenarios is based on how the characters are dressed. There are many relatively inexpensive costumes that you can purchase for these sexy roles. For better quality and more realistic clothing, you may need to shop around a bit more but you're sure to find some amazing products to suit any desire you have. These may be quite a bit more expensive. Another option is to make your own sexy costumes from clothing items obtained from a discount or secondhand store. With some creative remodelling and accessorizing, you can have even more fun crafting your alluring and seductive look from scratch. You can even design your naughty playtime outfits to come off easier when the time is right or provide more convenient access if you want to keep wearing them while having sex.

In many roleplay scenarios, pretending to be sexual strangers enhances the excitement. Creating this feeling of being completely new lovers experiencing sex for the first time together can be extremely hard. Your clothing choices can help to some degree but sometimes you may want even more of a disguise like wearing a wig, mask, different makeup or even body paint. Women may find this easier to do but guys can change their appearance just as easily. Also think of your other senses when trying to make yourself seem different. Consider a different perfume or cologne, shaving or waxing various parts of you body, penis extensions, body jewelry, flavoured lipstick, background sound tracks, etc. Making love in a novel location or even changing how your room looks (coloured lights, rearranging furniture, silk sheets, extra pillows) can also enhance the first time feeling.

The concept of fantasizing and roleplaying sex with other people may be troubling for some couples. Keep in mind that these scenarios are intended for adventurous couples who want more in their sex lives <u>without</u> venturing outside their committed relationship. It is intended to be a mutual experience that is fun and sexually rewarding for both of you. With this in mind, these should be fantasy treats rather than everyday experiences. Roleplaying should be a special event to complement your more traditional expressions of love and intimacy. Playing with your fantasies can help strengthen your emotional bonds but only if you have a good foundation of mutual trust, respect and love to begin with. Here are a few other guidelines to keep in mind when starting to explore your fantasies with roleplay:

- Keep an open mind and appreciate all the ideas your partner expresses with a genuine interest and sense of discovery

- Have fun and laugh together without ever laughing at or ridiculing each other

- Be aware of how your partner is reacting and be sensitive to their emotional state

- Always have a safe word to stop all play immediately if emotions or sensations become too intense

- Lower your expectations as to how your fantasies will play out in reality and be happily surprised when they're exceeded

- Allow yourselves to go with the flow even if it's not going exactly as you imagined or planned

- Even great actors need to rehearse, so give your fantasy roleplay sessions a few trial runs to improve your performance

- Some roleplay scenarios may never work out so just let them go and try some new ones

- Never make each other feel even a slight obligation to perform any role or activity

- Keep all personal fantasies and sexual desires private between the two of you alone

It's important to note that not all the fantasy ideas in this book are lovey-dovey type scenarios. Some are a little more risqué than others. In your roleplaying games you're free to fantasize about being and doing anything you want even if certain things just can't be done in reality (legally or physically impossible). You get to explore and experience wild sexual adventures in your imagination just for the mental thrill – it doesn't mean you want it to happen in real life or that you condone it being done to others. Combined with physical intimacy, these pretend roles can help intensify your sexual pleasure and emotional connection with your partner. Your roleplay games can be as wild and exotic as you want without worrying about historical accuracy or political sensitivity. They are your fantasies to explore privately as a couple. You can even adapt rigid sex laws or strict social customs from other countries to make your roleplay feel more forbidden and naughty. As long as you don't break the actual laws of your own country, you can make up your own rules to suit the way you want to play (please do read the Play Safe section).

However, keep in mind that strong emotional feelings may be triggered when you stretch your sexual comfort zone, cross certain boundaries or conflict with deeply held beliefs. For example, there are many BDSM related themes involving more intense activities such as bondage, punishment and forced sex fantasies that may provoke extreme feelings. Always have a unique safe word (orange, trout, spinach, etc.) or signal that you both agree upon at the start to halt everything immediately. And again, remember that not all fantasies need to be acted out fully. Sometimes you can just dress the part and let your imaginations run wild while making love. Just give your partner some clues as to how you want the sex to proceed – slow and tender or hard and fast. You can each have your own related but separate fantasies to play out in your own mind while enjoying each other physically.

Whatever way you want to play, it's a great time to embrace your fantasies and take your sex life to a whole new dimension. Pick a sexy scenario to start your erotic journey of discovery together. Feel free to swap the conventional male and female roles in any of the fantasy scenarios if it better suits your desires. The imaginary world you create for your adult play is under your total creative control so let your imagination loose, go wild and enjoy lots of hot, steamy sex with the one you love.

Sexy Scenario Sections

Here is a list of the various sections used to group the fantasy roleplay scenarios. The range of scenario numbers assigned to each set is also given so you can pick one semi-randomly based on just it's number.

Cougar Unleashed (1 to 10)

Lascivious Loving in the Library (11 to 19)

Babysitter Temptations (20 to 26)

Horny Hypnotists (27 to 30)

Crimes With Passion (31 to 35)

Frisky Business (36 to 50)

Maids, Masters & Mistresses (51 to 56)

Erotic Photography (57 to 61)

Staged Sex Scenes (62 to 66)

Like a Virgin (67 to 78)

Stranger Attraction (79 to 86)

Wild Westerns (87 to 92)

Tantalizing Times (93 to 97)

Fairy Tale Fantasies (98 to 111)

Wanton Witches & Wizards (112 to 119)

Voracious Vampires (120 to 123)

A complete list of all the scenario titles is available at the back of the book.

When you want to try your hand at coming up with your own creative roleplay ideas, give your erotic imagination a starting point with the mental topic triggers in the **Stimulating Hot Scenarios** section.

Communication is vital to any loving relationship. It's critical to achieving your sexual needs and for growing as an intimate couple together.

Develop a deeper intimacy with your lover by sharing thoughts and feelings openly. Quiet, intimate moments together are excellent times for sharing erotic dreams, desires and fantasies.

Cougar Unleashed

She's an upscale single lady living in a very private and exclusive gated community. Educated, sophisticated and confident, she worked hard to excel at her profession and succeed in business. Her wealth enables her to live a comfortable lifestyle with enough luxuries to keep her mostly happy. However, there were a few desires she suppressed and left unsatisfied until now. It's time to unleash her pent up lust and revel in the exquisite pleasures that her body has been craving for so long. Unfortunately most of the men in her social circles are either committed to a wife, business or another guy. But, the administration of her gated community offered a perk for single ladies they weren't even aware of. Every imaginable service was taken care of by a team of specialists. And, for security reasons, they provided a picture of all their staff for easy identification at the customer's door when they arrived. It was like they provided her with a catalog of potential playmates to fulfill all her fantasies. All she needed was a plausible reason to call for the type of help she desired. Being 'off limits' made the seduction even more thrilling for both her and her prey. There's no point having lot's of money if you can't enjoy some naughty fun with it.

Set the Scene
- Location: living room or bedroom
- Candlelight and wine set out for two
- Call your partner to make your help request and get an ETA
- Her Dress: elegant and sexy pencil dress or lingerie with stockings and high heels
- His Outfit: official looking uniform matching his role with an ID badge

Sexy Suggestions
- For Her: Use all your seductive charms to lure your prey into bed or where ever you desire. If he still resists, you can always threaten to turn him in for taking advantage of you. It's amazing what guys will do when their job and reputation are on the line - especially if it's something they'll enjoy anyway.
- For Him: Be as professional as possible while attempting to resist her advances. It's a tough job when your special services are in such demand but there are definitely some amazing benefits.

Personal Notes & Ideas

1 Fantasy Fireman

There's always a fireman posted on site for the fastest possible response to any emergency. And tonight, she's on fire burning with desire. She needs his special equipment and skills to properly handle her hot spots. Dressed in fiery red lingerie, she lights some candles and calls for help pretending that she smells smoke, has a trapped pussy or needs a fire safety inspection. As soon as the lone fireman arrives to assess the situation, he's overwhelmed with her sizzling heat - she's smoking hot. Seeing him dressed in uniform sets her passion a blaze. She swoons from the heat she feels and he rushes over to catch her. With his tank fully loaded and his hose primed for action, he gets to work. Will he need to call in backup?

- He can carry her to the sofa or bed and attend to her needs
- Enter her home through a window using a ladder
- She may want to inspect his hose and pumping engine
- He may need extra 'hose' (double dildo) to put out all her fires
- She could use his hose and practice with candles in the tub
- Finish with a fire extinguishing spray of foam

2 Pipe Cleaning Plumber

What better way to get her pipes flowing than to call a plumber and have them serviced professionally? She calls to request help with her clogged pipes and leaves a note on the door for the plumber to come up to the en suite of the master bedroom. She then soaks in a bubble bath eagerly waiting while pleasuring herself with a waterproof vibrator. He cautiously peaks into her bathroom and is surprised to see her relaxing in the tub with her eyes closed. A curious buzzing sound catches his attention just before she moans with pleasure. Captivated by the alluring sight, he watches her masturbate to orgasm. She smiles mischievously as she opens her eyes to catch him watching with an obvious sign of arousal. "Just in time" she says as she sits up exposing her breasts and motions for him to come in. Hesitantly he approaches and asks where the problem is. She reaches for his hand and guides it between her legs.

- She can insert a dildo and/or butt plug to be discovered
- She needs a big 'snake' to penetrate deep into her pipes
- Provide manual G-spot stimulation to get her juices really flowing (female ejaculation)
- Incorporate lube, anal beads and/or anal intercourse

3 Erotic Electrician

The lightening storm was a perfect opportunity to see if she could make sparks fly with the current electrician on call. She lit some candles then tripped all the breakers before calling for help. He arrived with a case of special 'tools' and supplies to handle any electrical situation. She greeted him at the door dressed in a silky teddy. An attractive charge was already building. As she led him into her great room, he noticed the two wine glasses on the coffee table but no one else seemed to be around. She followed his gaze and let him know she was all alone in the dark until now. "I was enjoying myself on the sofa while watching television when the lights went out" she informed him. He was mildly shocked when he noticed the porn movie case and plug in vibrator on the sofa. She smiled seductively and said "I wasn't able to finish and I'm still amped up. Can you help me?"

- Bring an assortment of battery powered sex toys
- "That's an amazing lightning rod you have"
- Investigate the new electro-stimulation sex toys

4 Randy Resident Responds

There's a clinic on site that's open 24x7 offering various diagnostic and treatment options. A few medical residents also gain more experience and financial rewards by making house calls. Feeling a little tense, she looks to see who's on call. She catches her breath and feels her heart race when his picture comes up on screen. His eyes and smile made her knees feel weak and certain parts of her body tingle with desire. She calls and describes her condition: tense muscles, feeling weak, shortness of breath, racing heart, regional throbbing and tingling. The doctor in training is dispatched immediately with instructions to see his patient in her bedroom. She's looking forward to his touch as he performs a full body exam. And forget bedside manners, she wants him misbehaving in her bed.

- "I'll need you to remove your top. It's okay I'm a doctor."
- "You have all the signs of being horny bordering on hysteria."
- "There's only one known cure. You need an orgasm stat."
- "I'll write you a sex prescription and personally give you a testosterone injection vaginally."
- Bring a doctor's bag filled with vibrating and probing instruments

5 Police Protection

It's late at night when a noise wakes her from a very erotic dream. Now that she's awake, every sound seems magnified and extra creepy. Getting back to her dream or even fantasizing about it while masturbating isn't going to happen. She needs some police protection to calm her nerves. Being wrapped in the strong arms of a police officer would definitely help relieve the mounting tension she was feeling. She calls for help to investigate a possible break in. The officer arrives and performs a thorough search while she clings to his arm. The combination of her revealing lingerie and feel of her gorgeous body pressing against him had the desired effect. Her bedroom was the last place to investigate. Gazing seductively into his eyes, she says "I'm all alone and scared. Please stay and help me get to sleep. I'll feel so much better while you're here with your big, hard night stick."

- "Thanks for arriving so quickly - I hope you don't come as fast."
- "Officer, I'll do *anything* you want if you stay."
- "Well it is my duty to protect and serve."

6 Masseur With Magic Fingers

Browsing through the community services website for options available to satisfy her fantasies, she discovers they offer in home massage treatment for medical and relaxation purposes. She wouldn't even need a ruse to order this service. The picture of the masseur on call made her shiver in delight as she imagined his hands caressing her entire body. He came prepared with a bundle of soft towels, a selection of massage oils, a portable sound system and a case of special massage aids. With her undressed and partially covered with a sheet, he starts with her head, neck and back. As she relaxes she can't help but sigh and moan with pleasure from his sensual touch. He's getting turned on too and, knowing the effect he is having on her, his fingers work their magic on more intimate areas of her body. He's sure to get a big tip tonight.

- Enjoy an extended breast and nipple massage with lube
- Give her an orgasm with manual stimulation
- Caress her entire body with selected vibrators
- Check out some erotic massage books for stimulating techniques

7 Hands on Handyman

She had hired him before to fence in her backyard around the pool. Unfortunately he was with a crew of other guys so she had to settle for admiring his body and fantasizing. But today he was working on her deck alone. His muscles gleamed in the sun. As she watched him work, she became even more horny for this handyman. She had always been around men using their minds mostly so a man performing physical labour seemed to bring out her primal sexual urges. His rugged character combined with the smell of fresh sawdust and the rhythmic pounding of his hammer made her ache with desire. Even the way he handled his wood - she wanted him to grab her, man handle her, work on her, lay her, screw her and hammer away until she was properly nailed. She didn't even care if he split her with his huge spike. She invites him in for a cool drink … and hot sex.

- Talk dirty with lots of erotic handyman related euphemisms
- Focus on vigorous, passionate sex with lots of energy
- Enjoy sex standing up, bent over a table or while being picked up

8 Erotic Exercise Instructor

At the gym she noticed a personal trainer 'motivating' a woman to work harder and faster. That night, she couldn't get the submissively erotic thoughts of being 'trained' by him out of her mind. She arranged for a personal session with him at home in her exercise room. When she let him in their eyes locked for a brief instant before she had to look away. There was an immediate and powerful connection between them. She felt that he knew exactly what she wanted even more than she did herself. He was going to work her hard until she was hot and dripping wet. She led him into her exercise room and then he informed her "We must train in the nude." He then commanded her to "undress now!" as he proceeded to remove his clothing as well. First he has her stretch and pose in different positions to feel her muscle tone and flexibility. He then introduces her to his own special pole exercises - thrusts, lunges, squats, push ups, sit ups, butt crunches and others that will work her entire body.

- Who says sex only uses a few hundred calories
- Try every position possible where she controls and performs the motion
- See how many regular exercises you can transform for sex
- He constantly encourages her to go faster, harder, deeper
- Use a suction cup dildo on the floor/wall/bench if required to 'stand in'
- Use a blowup exercise ball in part of your routine

9 Strict Sheriff

He's patrolling the neighbourhood in an unmarked car and can't help but notice her as she walks to her door, unlocks it and disappears inside. Parked on the side of the road, he lets his fantasies run wild. Just as he's imagining all the kinky things he'd love to do with this hot sexy lady, dispatch radios a call about a possible burglary. Apparently a woman found her front door open when she arrived home. When he obtained the address he immediately knew something was fishy. Getting out of the car, he walked up to her house. "Wow! That was fast" she exclaimed when she opened the door for the sheriff. "I was close by so I took the call." Surveying the situation, he knew what she was up to but she was going to be in for a surprise. He started asking her some tough questions to put her off guard and make her a bit nervous. After making her squirm a bit, he announces "I know you're lying and I'm going to have to arrest you for making this fake burglary report. Up against the wall and spread your legs so I can frisk you." Terrified, she complies but begs him "Don't take me to jail Sheriff, I'll do anything you want." He handcuffs her then says "You're going to get what you deserve and I know just what you need."

- "A good spanking might teach you a lesson."
- "On your knees, hands behind your back."
- "I'm going to have to punish you with my night stick."

10 Frisky With The French Maid

Many of her masturbation fantasies curiously involved having sex with another woman. Whenever she scanned the community services brochure for hot staff members, she always paused at the French maid advertisement but then moved on to the guys. However tonight, the thought of having a maid service her every whim made her pussy wet with desire. She found the look of the frilly black and white uniform erotically exciting. Her craving to dominate another woman fueled her fantasies even more.

- Let your guy watch as you make out with another woman
- Have him dress up as a maid and bend to your wishes
- She receives oral pleasuring then uses a strap-on for the maid
- The maid receives a sensual spanking if tasks are not done right

Lascivious Loving in the Library

The library represents the conflict in all of us regarding our sexuality. On the surface it's prim and proper where you're expected to follow the rules and be quiet. Yet it's also the source of carnal knowledge and inspiration for all sorts of erotic fantasies. You're expected to suppress your urges even as you're fuelling your desires. But, like a pressure cooker, repressed sexuality just makes it hotter and more steamy. The forbidden becomes even more seductive and tantalizing. As the sexual heat builds, it's even more exciting when you break through the facade of innocence and propriety to unleash the fiery passion and lust hidden from view. In these scenarios, the library provides the setting where temptation culminates in orgasmic ecstasy.

Set the Scene
- Location: library/bookstore (if you dare), den or living room
- Reading sofa, sturdy desk or study table and bookshelves
- Ensure the room is quiet and tidy
- Female Librarian: tight pencil skirt, button down shirt, stockings, heels, hair done up, horn-rimmed glasses
- Male Librarian: sophisticated semi-formal sport jacket or vest with tie
- A variety of sex books (manuals, pictorials, erotica)

Sexy Suggestions
- Use proper grammar and a sophisticated vocabulary to start then transition to slang and dirty talk when things heat up
- Even when the action and passion escalates, keep as quiet as you can for fear of getting caught
- Dress sexy while looking prim and proper or innocent according to the role

Personal Notes & Ideas

11 Front Desk Fantasy

It was a slow night and she didn't expect anyone else to show up tonight. She took a quick look around but didn't see him sitting on the floor behind a shelf of books. Thinking she was alone, she locked the door and, just in case someone showed up, put up a sign with a note that said she was busy and to ring for service. This was her time to enjoy herself with a good book. And the one she recently found was a juicy one. She settled down behind her desk and started reading. Absorbed in the erotic story, she started stroking her nipples swelling with excitement beneath her silky top. Meanwhile, the guy with a secret crush on the librarian got up to leave and spied her. Fascinated, he slowly and quietly approached so he didn't disturb her fantasy. He watched as she leaned her head back, closed her eyes and let her hand stray down between her legs. Just as she was about to bring herself to orgasm, the closing time chime sounded. Startled, she opened her eyes to see him standing in front of her desk. He blurted out "Sorry to disturb you but I noticed we're both reading the same book and I think you're so hot." Seeing the erection in his pants, she let her hair down and climbed on the desk to grab him.

- Set a timer and watch her masturbate until it goes off
- Ravish each other on the desk or with her bent over it
- Describe erotic scenes in the book as you're having sex

12 Banned Book Buyer

Working at her desk, she raised her head up to see a stern but attractive looking man staring at her cleavage. He informed her that he was the trustee in charge of moral decency for all the libraries in the district. "I am here on official business. It appears this library has come into the possession of a large number of prohibited books. It seems you've been ordering these banned books a few at a time from restricted publishers hoping we wouldn't discover them." He could see she was getting nervous as she blushed and squirmed in her chair. "Follow me" he ordered as he led her to the Antique Books room. It was normally locked but he had the key. Just as he suspected, she had amassed quite a collection of books on sex from erotic art to pornographic fiction. They were from various ages and countries too. "You realize you could be fired for this" he threatened. "Please sir, I am at your mercy. I beg your forgiveness. Isn't there something I can do to make this right?" she pleaded. "Hmmm, although it's the righteous thing to do, it would be a shame to burn these books and tarnish your career. Maybe there's another way to punish you" he said with a wicked grin. "And I'm sure, after reading all these books, you know a few ways to help me overlook this transgression."

- Give her a spanking while she reads out loud from an erotic story
- Have her pick a book, turn to a random page and perform the sex act

13 Strapping Jock Support

All through her high school years, she had lusted after the strapping young athletes in her classes. She fantasized about losing her virginity to more than one of them but they were never interested in her. Although she was a socially inept, nerdy geek back then, they didn't have to be so mean. However, now that she was done college, she was smoking hot, sexually confident and much smarter too. And, as librarian and head of the academic standards committee at her old high school, she had the authority to teach these jocks a lesson. Each student she selected for personal tutoring would do as they were told - they needed her support to stay on the team. While they were going to love learning her way, she was going to use her power to satisfy her fantasies and enjoy some kinky fun at the same time. And with her dominatrix training, she'd be able to easily whip them into shape for any position she desired.

- What's she going to do with that tight end?
- Give him a human biology lesson with 'tip of the tongue' testing
- Make history interesting by focusing on sex and debauchery throughout the ages
- Learn to appreciate erotic art and maybe create some of your own

14 Power Outage Overture

When the thunder and lightning started off in the distance, most people quickly went home. But for some reason, one woman stayed and continued looking through a stack of books. She was very attractive and he kept watching her surreptitiously. The storm was getting more intense and he knew the power was likely to go out any minute so he quickly rounded up a flashlight and some candles. Then, just as he anticipated, the lights flickered and died. The darkness was pitch black - even the emergency lights failed to come on. He heard her gasp. Turning on the flashlight he called out to her "please stay where you are. Don't move … I'm coming." When he arrived at her table, he noticed the pile of sex manuals she was looking through. Even in the faint lighting, he could tell she was blushing. "Don't feel embarrassed" he reassured her "I've read all of these myself. The storm sounds like it's getting worse so it'll be much safer for us to remain here. Since this may last a few hours at least, would you like to join me in my study. I have a bottle of wine we could share and a private collection of books you might find interesting."

- Turn off all the lights, use candlelight to look at erotic art books together
- Talk about the pictures and make up sexual fantasies to turn each other on
- Pretend you're both still virgins experiencing sex vicariously through books until tonight

15 Salacious Magic Spells

He noticed her as she quietly slipped into the library and headed toward the "New Age" section. She was obviously upset about something. He hoped it was about some guy she was in love with. She was still dressed in her Catholic girls school uniform so he knew why she had come here instead of the school library. Desperation was leading her to the "dark side". He wasn't sure if she was still a virgin but he remotely activated the secret compartment and locked the door just in case. As if by magic, a concealed section of the bookshelf opened when she moved in front of it. Inside was a scroll with a spell he obtained from an ancient book of black magic called Incubus Incantations and Succubus Spells. Curiosity would surely make her read this deceptively written love spell. Promising her the power to seduce the man of her dreams, it was really just half of a deviously lecherous lust spell. If she was pure and read it aloud, her sexual desires and fantasies would redirect to the person reading the second half of the spell. He had that part memorized.

- Make up your own love spell scroll
- She can be innocent while eagerly craving his touch
- She can become lust crazed and ravish him

16 Head Master

She was sent to his office for reading inappropriate and immoral material in class. The story was just getting to the juicy part too but now she was squirming in his leather chair while he slowly flipped through her book. Just as he was about to lace into her, he was called out. She was left alone to anxiously await her punishment with the 'bench' in plain sight. The thought made her butt tingle with both dread and excitement. She got up and paced to relieve the tension building inside her. Walking toward his bookcase, she noticed a crack along the edge. With the lightest of touch, the bookcase swung out to reveal a private den. It was filled with nude statues, erotic paintings and hundreds of sex books. Forgetting the trouble she was already in, she entered the room enthralled with the sexual imagery. Without knowing it, he had returned and was watching her just as she opened a book on fellatio. She started reading the instructions for performing a blow job. When she finished, he surprised her by saying "it appears you have the desire to become a head master. It'll be a pleasure giving you a good lesson."

- She should dress in a school girl outfit with a short skirt
- He gives her instructions for giving great head
- A spanking or paddling is the punishment for doing it wrong

17 Ladies Night at the Library

He found it odd that they would shut down the entire library for a group of women to meet every other week with no men allowed. Out of curiosity he decided to hide out and see what they were up too. A number of well dressed, wealthy women arrived, locked the doors, lowered all the window blinds and gathered around a large table. After setting out some wine and lighting a number of candles, they turned off the lights and brought out their books. From his vantage point, he could see they were all of an erotic nature. This wasn't just a book club, it was carnal coven. They started reading their favourite passages and revealing their dirtiest fantasies. He was getting turned on but growing an erection while laying on his stomach was a big problem. Trying to readjust, he accidentally knocked over a book. The loud thud got everyone's attention - now he was really in trouble. All the ladies grabbed him and somehow tied him to a chair with scarves. After blindfolding him, they decided to have some frisky female fun.

- In candlelight, read an erotic story or female sex fantasies out loud while he listens
- After he is tied and blindfolded, she can pretend to be different women taking turns
- Alter how you normally perform various sex play activities, wear different tops, change hair styles, add lipstick or spray on a new perfume to make him believe you could be another woman
- Give him a drink of wine suggesting it is a memory alteration potion

18 Perverted Purity Pledge

The sorority was extremely popular and she was desperate to get in. They were also very well connected and powerful for reasons she was about to discover. All the pledges were gathered anxiously waiting for the ceremony to begin. The head mistress addressed the girls. "Ladies, tonight you will prove your worthiness to join our sorority by demonstrating your feminine powers. You have already passed the first test by providing us with your wildest masturbation videos. By successfully completing our second, specially designed seduction challenge, you'll discover how to get whatever you desire in life. You'll also be helping us consolidate our influence in the community. In this bag, we've put the names of various married men who are in positions we want to control." All the girls reached into the bag to pick a name which was then recorded next to theirs in a large leather journal. "Your task is to seduce and have sex with your target on camera. But, there are only 13 spots available. To gain entry, you must film him doing the most kinky, nasty, obscene and perverted sex acts possible. The entire sorority will judge your performances. We will also be keeping all your videos to ensure your secrecy even if you don't win." For reasons she didn't understand yet, her target was the university librarian.

- He's prim, proper and married so will resist her temptations initially
- She can dress innocent or slutty depending on a desired style of seduction
- Use a real video camera if desired or pretend you are being filmed in secret

19 Reading Room Romp

She saw him sitting alone on the couch in the reading room with one of her favourite erotic novels in his hands. It was getting late and he was the only one left besides herself. He was a regular and always smiled at her when they passed by each other. Everything about him was sexy but his eyes were especially gorgeous. When he looked at her in that certain way, her pussy ached with desire. And, as he walked down the aisles, she would always turn around to watch his butt and fantasize what it would feel like to grab his ass while he was thrusting between her legs. While she secretly watched him read, she noticed a large bulge grow in his pants. Then his hand drifted down to half hide and half stroke his enormous erection. Without hesitation she knew what she had to do. She was going to bring the story to life for both of them.

- Have wild and energetic sex on the couch
- Re-enact a sex scene from an erotic story
- She can be a librarian, student or visitor

Sex does not need to be performed completely naked. Add a bit of style by incorporating a few erotic accessories. Aesthetically pleasing or functional, the right accessory can make sex even more special.

Accessories include jewelry, clothing or costumes, toys, food, symbolic or fetish objects, props, art or anything that enhances the setting. Make sex both playful and aesthetically pleasing.

Babysitter Temptations

Babysitters are usually sweet, young and innocent looking so you can trust them with your children. However, they are also at the age where they are experiencing raging hormones and stirring sexual desires. The age difference between the adult and babysitter makes it a social taboo that only intensifies the excitement. The temptation to fulfill the fantasy combined with its forbidden nature creates an erotic tension that fuels the desire even more. There is also the element of cheating on a partner that makes the attraction feel even more illicit. The sitter is young and sexually inexperienced while the adult is more skilled, knowledgable and confident. You just need the right opportunity to explore these naughty feelings without "getting caught".

Set the Scene
* Location: couch, bedroom or in the car
* Babysitter should dress innocent but attractive
* Adult should dress semi-formal as if returning from work or an evening out on the town
* Pretend the kids are asleep when you arrive home
* Condoms even if you don't use them anymore
* Use a new type of perfume or cologne
* Some actual cash to pay the sitter

Sexy Suggestions
* If you plan to have sex in the car, scout a secluded place to park ahead of time
* Ask the sitter about their love interest or secret crush to get a sex conversation started
* Mix in memories of your own high school days and naughty things you did when younger
* The sitter should perform and react as if sex with a skilled lover is totally new
* You can slyly initiate this type of roleplay while driving home with your partner

Personal Notes & Ideas

20 Learning to Drive Stick

She wanted to stay out later and have some more fun but his game was on and he just had to watch it. Driving the sitter home was now up to her so she could still go out for a bit longer if she desired. As the sitter stood up to leave with her, she scanned his lean body and felt a strange sense of sexual excitement that she hadn't felt in a long time. An explicit mental image of her riding his hard cock flashed through her mind. She smiled at him as he walked by to get his shoes. She snatched a quick look at his ass when he bent over to tie them. When she walked out the door, she yelled to her husband that she was going out for a drive. In the car, she drove quietly for a minute sensually stroking the stick shift then looked at him, sweetly smiled and asked "You have your learners permit don't you? Would you like me to teach you to drive?" She pulled onto a side road and parked the car. "But first, I need to teach you how to properly use this stick" she whispered seductively in his ear as she stroked her fingers along the bulge in his pants.

- "I've seen you looking at my *headlights*. Let me show you how to turn them on."
- "You can't drive with that huge erection. I'll have to help you get it into gear."
- Take a joy ride in the back seat and let him feel her engine purr
- She can teach him how to get her into gear manually then get his piston working

21 Overtime Bonus

His wife was out of town so he took a few days off to look after the kids. As fortune would have it, there was an urgent matter at work that he was called in to resolve. With such short notice, he was lucky that their standard sitter was still available. She arrived and he quickly left so he could get back as fast as possible. He was glad he went in because he was rewarded with a huge bonus. When he got back home, the kids were already sound asleep. The sitter started getting ready to leave when he suggested she stay to help him celebrate his bonus with a toast. She accepted and as he was pouring a glass of wine for her, she casually mentioned "I sure could use some extra money for school." And then with a flirtatious smile, she seductively asked "Are there any jobs I can do for you while your wife is away?" He had always fantasized about her so was instantly aroused by her suggestive request. "Well, off the top of my head, an idea just popped up."

- Negotiate a bonus for a blow job or hand job
- For the right price he could take her virginity
- Make sure you are both super quiet so you don't wake the kids

22 Smuggled in to Snuggle

When her mom's friend called her to babysit, she was ecstatic. The couple was rich, had an amazing house and they paid her really well. However there was another reason for her excitement. She was getting serious with her boyfriend but there was nowhere they could be alone. This was her chance to be together with him and maybe even kiss. Her make out fantasies sometimes led to sex when she was playing with herself but just snuggling in his arms while watching a movie would be wonderful. The couple were going to the opera then to an after show party so they would be out until early morning. They even put their kids to sleep before leaving so she had at least four hours to be alone with her boyfriend. She waited a while to make sure the couple didn't forget something and come back. When she thought it was safe, she opened the back door to let him in.

- How far will she go and what will they do for the first time together?
- Will they stay on the couch or venture to the master bedroom?
- Do they discover the couple's lingerie, sex books, dirty movies or sex toys?

23 Home by Midnight

His wife was feeling tired so they decided to go home early. She went straight to bed and fell asleep almost immediately. After checking on the kids, he went down stairs to take the babysitter home. Lately he felt a little uneasy around her especially now that she had grown into a very attractive young woman. He also had the distinct impression that she was flirting with him. Although he hoped it was just an innocent infatuation, the thought that she wanted him was a huge boost to his ego. Mental images of having sex with her also made his fantasies extra hot. Just as they were getting close to her home, she said "I have to be home by midnight but it's still early. Can we go somewhere quiet to talk? There are some things I need to ask a man that I can't talk to my dad about." His mind raced with the implications of her request but he drove right by her house.

- When he parks the car and turns off the engine, she leans over and whispers that she loves the smell of his cologne while reaching to unzip his pants
- She tells him she wants to have sex with an experienced man who can show her how to have an orgasm for the first time
- After he tells her how to give a him a blow job, he introduces her to the sensual pleasures of cunnilingus, helps her find her G-spot then lets her ride him in the back seat

24 Mistress Bedroom Mischief

The contract negotiations were finished much earlier than anticipated so she booked a flight to get home a few days earlier than planned. In the rush to leave, she forgot to phone her house sitter to let him know. He was there to look after her dog but she knew he was going to be enjoying himself in her condo. He was the shy studious type just starting university so she trusted he wasn't going to be throwing any wild parties. When she opened the door, her dog greeted her happily but the sitter wasn't around. The television was on and his books were open on the table so she assumed he was around close by somewhere. Deciding to put her luggage away before looking for him, she opened her bedroom door to find him on her bed dressed in her lingerie. He even had on her wig, lipstick, stockings and heels. Blushing with embarrassment, he froze unable to say a word. With a wicked smile, she closed the door and said "I think I'm going to have some fun with you and you better play along if you want this kept secret."

- "First I think you need to be punished for being in my room without permission."
- "Then you're going to give me a good licking just like you would want your *pussy* licked."
- "I purchased this strap-on a while ago and now I have a good reason to use it."

25 Dirty Dreams Come True

When he found out his parents were leaving for a week long vacation, his mind drifted to one of his favourite fantasies. He feigned disappointment that they arranged a sitter supposedly for the house. However, secretly he hoped they invited his mom's close friend to look after him. She had a daughter about his age just starting college but he wasn't interested in her. The hot and super sexy mother was the one starring in his dirty dreams. She'd been to the house many times as he was growing up. Just thinking about her gave him an instant hard on. She arrived shortly after his parents left for the airport. He answered the door to find that she was more gorgeous than ever. She hugged him then looked him up and down. "You've grown into a very handsome young man" she said with a smile. "I'm so glad to see you again" she continued as she reached out to stroke his face. She then glanced down, noticed the bulge in his pants and said "It looks like you're very happy to see me too."

- "Let's get you inside and I'll show you how I can take care of that for you."
- She can take charge and teach this eager student how to pleasure a woman
- He can try to prove his virility by using all the moves he's rehearsed in his fantasies

26 Teddy Bear Confessions

With all the awful events in the news, his wife was paranoid about leaving the kids with a sitter. To alleviate her fears, he installed wireless cameras throughout the house - except for the bedroom much to his disappointment. They were very well hidden. He even put a few in the kid's teddy bears. His wife was leery about going out that night but it was her promotion party so she was expected to be there. They had used the babysitter a few times before and they took separate cars so he could leave at any time to check up on them. The kids were already asleep so all she had to do was entertain herself for a few hours. As they were leaving, the sitter locked eyes with him for a brief instant. He was struck with an overwhelming feeling of mutual attraction and desire. At the party, he stepped outside to check the cameras with his smart phone. As he flicked through each of the cameras, he was shocked to see the teddy cam showing a hot sexy young woman in the master bedroom on his bed. She was dressed in his wife's lingerie, masturbating, calling out his name and saying how much she wanted him deep inside her. He couldn't stop watching until she reached orgasm and then started to clean up. He quickly made some excuse that he was going to check on the sitter and left for home.

- "A little bear told me some naughty things about you tonight. Is any of it true?"
- "I just came home to check on the hidden cameras. Would you like to make *another* movie with me this time?"
- Make a masturbation video for him to watch before having fun together. Include a hot sexual fantasy involving him.

The type and style of clothing we wear affects our mood and behaviour as well as those around us. Rather than being completely naked when making love, try wearing different types or amounts of clothing to make sex more exciting.

Consider different styles: lingerie, business, classy, elegant, slutty or fetish. Combine various clothing styles to enhance your mental and physical stimulation. Use your normal clothes or buy special outfits just for your adult playtime.

Horny Hypnotists

With the ability to place their subjects into a highly suggestive state, hypnotists have the power to encourage you to follow their directions. They can bypass your conscious control to access hidden and sensitive regions of your subconscious that you may not even be aware of. Access to your inner mind gives them the keys to all your desires, fantasies and memories with the potential to unlock secrets that can help resolve issues in your life. While hypnotized you lose voluntary control however it's claimed that you cannot be made to do anything you don't want to do. If you are the one being hypnotized, what would you be willing to do when your inhibitions have been lowered? And, if you are an unethical hypnotist, what would you want your subject to do to demonstrate your power over them? What radical cure will you devise to help your client improve their condition?

Set the Scene
- Location: a home office, den or living room
- Start in a formal manner asking a number of questions
- Couch or recliner chair for the subject to relax on
- Read a guided hypnosis or relaxation script
- Remind the subject they will not remember a thing and that they will awake happy, refreshed and satisfied
- Quiet instrumental music playing in the background
- Hypnotist should dress professionally
- A pocket watch to initiate the state of hypnosis
- Throw pillows
- A variety of sex toys hidden in a drawer

Sexy Suggestions
- Have them describe their ultimate sexual fantasies in explicit detail
- Ask questions about their sexual history and first time they had sex
- Explore the limits of their sexual comfort zone and what they consider forbidden or taboo
- Test your subject's level of hypnosis by getting them to do or say progressively more embarrassing things
- See how far you can go before their deepest inhibitions stop them from responding to your commands

Personal Notes & Ideas

27 Unrelenting Sexual Urges

She appeared to be a shy and virtuous young lady with a look of innocence and purity. However, her moral behaviour in public hid the turmoil of sexual urges she experienced constantly. She fought hard to suppress the erotic images and thoughts of sex that invaded her mind. When she met people throughout the day, she would have visions of them engaging in sex either with her, by themselves or with others around them. She felt troubled that these fantasies aroused her so much. The only way she could stop them (at least for a little while) was to quickly find a secluded spot to relieve herself manually. Once or twice used to be enough to get her through the day but lately she needed almost hourly relief. Desperate to find a way to control her lustful desires, she went to see a hypnotist. He eagerly accepted the challenge to find the source of her chronic arousal syndrome.

- To better understand her condition, ask her to describe in explicit detail the kinds of fantasies she encounters
- Under hypnosis, have her demonstrate her self relief techniques
- Discover that her masturbation sessions never result in orgasm (she stops herself just on the verge of climax every time)
- Initiate your professional treatment option while she is still under your power

28 Hot & Frigid

She was hot and sexy with no lack of men or even women trying to get into her pants. However, even though she adored the attention and wanted to fall in love, she could not bring herself to have sex. It wasn't that she didn't want to. She even had explicit sexual fantasies but when it came right down to it, she refused to give in to her burning desires. She couldn't even touch herself let alone pleasure herself to orgasm. There had to be a reason for her inhibition toward sex. She knew she wasn't crazy but there had to be some kind of mental block that was making her frigid. Maybe she was afraid of losing control if she had an orgasm. Doing some research online she found that people could be made to orgasm under hypnosis. She was eager to find out if this kind of technique could help her. She booked an appointment and even signed a waiver regarding the unconventional sexual treatment she was about to receive. She was willing to do anything and everything to open herself for sex. The hypnotist promised he would fire up her passion and enable her to have a normal love life.

- Under hypnosis, instruct her to show you different parts of her body and stimulate herself with a feather then her fingers
- Explore how she reacts to her self stimulation then pleasure her yourself using various foreplay techniques
- Reveal different parts of your own body and instruct her to pleasure you in various ways
- Manually or orally stimulate her to orgasm while encouraging her to visualize the pleasure as warm waves washing over ice until it melts
- Give her positive suggestions regarding the use of vibrators and dildos and encourage her to try using them
- Complete the treatment by instructing her to get into her favourite position for intercourse and to beg you to give it to her

29 Command & Control Challenge

She was a university student majoring in psychology and just received a special course in hypno-therapy. Her professor even gave her the opportunity to practice under his guidance with a group of student volunteers. From the results, she appeared to have a natural talent for hypnotizing people and received a certificate acknowledging her completion of the course with high honers. She couldn't wait to tell her boyfriend. Unfortunately he wasn't very supportive of her achievement. Dismissing hypnosis as nonsense, he ridiculed the therapeutic benefits. He then joked about all the perverted things he would get women to do if he had the power to hypnotize them. Claiming only weak minded people could be made to do those kinds of silly things, he boasted that no one would ever be able to hypnotize him. She thought to herself, sure some people are not susceptible to hypnosis, but he wasn't one of them. She challenged him to let her try to hypnotize him and he accepted. When he was under her command and control, she was going to make him do her bidding and then maybe change a few of his habits in bed.

- What kinds of kinky things could she make him do or say that would prove he wasn't faking it?
- Start off slow and see how much fun you can have getting him to perform wildly erotic tasks for you
- Give him suggestions for pleasuring you in ways you always wanted and get him to practice then and there

30 Think Straight

He was sure a few people suspected but he hadn't come out yet. Although all his erotic desires were fueled by thoughts of other men, he loved the company of women and desperately wanted a way to find them sexually attractive too. According to a lot of "experts", being gay was a choice or a way of thinking that could be corrected. Supposedly all he had to do was think straight and everything would be fine. But it wasn't working no matter how hard he tried. Just when he was thinking of giving up, he spotted an ad for a hypnotist who claimed she could help anyone adjust their sexual preferences and enjoy a "normal" love life. She claimed to have a radical new therapy that could transform a person's sexual mindset in as little as one session. Everything was confidential and her services came with a money back guarantee. He eagerly called to discuss his problem and make an appointment. When he showed up at her office, he was surprised to see the therapist dressed as a man. The room also looked more like a bedroom complete with a large bed. Noticing his bewilderment, she calmly reassured him that this was all part of her program and offered him a seat. She explained that she would hypnotize him and then progressively lead him through various sexual scenarios. To suppress initial resistance, she would start by appealing to his current desires. As the session progressed, she would transform her appearance and behaviour to be more feminine. While in a suggestive trance, these sexual activities would create new erotic pleasure associations and help attune his mind to desire women.

- Initially dress as a man with your hair done up
- Pretend to hypnotize your partner with the initial suggestion that you are gay lovers
- Start with some male oriented foreplay leading to fellatio
- At various stages, pause the session and reveal or add more feminine features (let your hair down, add lipstick, spray on some perfume, remove clothing, change a male item of clothing for a female version, etc.)
- Continue in this way until you are both fully naked enjoying intercourse
- Add in strap-on or double dildo play if desired
- Wake the subject with a final sexy suggestion and schedule another appointment
- Switch roles playing with a male hypnotist and a female client

Crimes With Passion

As portrayed in movies and television, criminal activities, situations and personalities can provide many interesting ideas for exciting sex play involving dominant and submissive roles. These kinds of roleplay themes also present opportunities to explore elements of bondage and captivity. Playing a bad boy or girl willing to break the rules and take what you want can be thrilling. You can even wear a mask to hide your identity and allow your super villain alter ego to come out to play. Being a pretend victim can also be emotionally exciting. And of course, with crime comes interrogation and punishment if you get taken into custody. Even petty criminals risk the consequences of being caught in the act and being forced to do things to avoid jail time.

Set the Scene
- Location: bedroom, darkened room, back alley, van
- Burglar: all black cat suit, mask and gloves
- Duct tape, rope, handcuffs, fake gun, rubber knife
- Police attire: night stick, handcuffs, uniform, badge
- Biker or gang member: leather, sun glasses, bandanna, fake tattoos

Sexy Suggestions
- Communicate with each other when your roleplay scene is going to take place to ensure it's not going to be mistaken for the real thing
- Sexual favours can be traded for your freedom or taken "forcefully"
- Sexually compromising photos can be taken to ensure compliance and secrecy

Personal Notes & Ideas

31 Intimate Intruder

After casing the place for weeks, he wasn't expecting her to be home but there she was in bed sound asleep. In his line of work, he was prepared for anything. All he wanted were the jewels in her safe but it was going to take some time to crack so he had to tie her up. He had special bondage equipment just for this kind of situation. He woke her by covering her mouth with his hand to stop her from screaming. To make her more submissive he aggressively threatened her to do as she was told and proceeded to restrain her spread eagled on the bed. Now for the jewelry. With skillful fingers he unlocked the safe only to discover a collection of high end glass dildos and sexual accessories. She must be hiding her gems somewhere else and he knew exactly how to make her talk. He wasn't a violent man but, with her toys and his finger skills, he would be able to make her squirm until she couldn't take it anymore. This job was going to be a pleasure for both of them.

- "Let's see if I can find the combination to unlock your orgasmic potential."
- "I'm going to make you come so many times you're going to beg me to stop."
- "I feel bad taking everything. I think I'll leave you with a nice pearl necklace."

32 Lingerie Lifting

Normally a female security guard monitored the hidden cameras in the dressing rooms but he was called in last minute to cover her shift. As he scanned the video screens, he couldn't believe his luck as he watched all the hot women come in, strip down and try on all the sexy clothing the stored had on sale. It was his job to keep a close eye on the ladies to ensure none of the clothing left the store on their bodies. One attractive woman caught his attention when she stripped down, admired herself in the mirrors then tried on a selection of very erotic lingerie. When she found one she seemed to like, she caressed herself sensually and tweaked her nipples to see how they looked poking through the material. He couldn't help getting aroused watching her pleasure herself. Unfortunately when she was done, she just slipped on her dress over the merchandise, put the undesired items back and walked out of the store. He quickly ran out of his office to apprehend her before she could escape. Sneaking up behind her, he grabbed her arm and said "You are under arrest for shop lifting. I want you to come with me." He escorted her back to his office, restrained her to a chair then locked the door. He then sat down at his desk to discuss her crime and punishment options.

- Brief her about the consequences including possible jail time
- Delicately strip the stolen items from her body as evidence
- She pleads for anyway to avoid harsh punishment
- Buy some new lingerie leaving the price tags on to be discovered
- Play in an office type setting and have sex on the desk or standing up against the wall

33 Erotic Spy Exchange

He saw her walking toward him in her trench coat and high heels. She was the courier for their clandestine operation. As she came closer, he flashed her a warning sign that something wasn't right. He had the feeling that they were under surveillance so rather than a straight exchange, they would need to act as if they were having a secret affair. There was no other explanation for the two of them to be in this secluded location. They must have tapped his phone and flagged a conversation with the word missile in it. Thinking it would be best to hide in plain sight, he quickly embraced and kissed her passionately. While hugging her, he whispered in her ear that they needed to have sex and refer to his penis as a missile to throw off suspicion. It would also be the perfect cover to slip two small metal balls containing the projectile guidance chips into her secret hiding place. Before she could speak, he opened his coat and said "I have the missile prototype right here in my pants for your inspection." Without missing a beat, she knelt down to get a closer look and, as she took it in her hands, she exclaimed "Wow, it must be capable of delivering a very powerful thrust."

- See how many missile related sexual euphemisms you can use while having sex
- After intercourse, surreptitiously insert two ben-wa balls

34 Condition for Release

He was a probation officer who seemed to attract a lot of female cases. In his position of power he discovered that he could receive sexual favours if he was willing to overlook minor infractions. No one wanted to be sent back to prison especially for some minor lapse so, depending on the violation, they would usually offer it directly or give in to a bit of pressure. However, there was one woman he was very attracted to but she never seemed to break the rules or at least was clever enough not to get caught yet. She was almost finished her sentence and would be released soon but he had a different kind of release in mind for both of them. She was under house arrest with a very strict curfew setup so she could work. He decided that an unscheduled visit for a surprise inspection might reveal something interesting. As luck would have it, he arrived when she was supposed to be home but she was late. She seemed shocked and a little nervous as she let him in. The first thing he noticed was an empty glass and a half finished bottle of wine on the table. He explained what he was doing there and identified all the rules she had broken as he looked around. Although most were trivial, he exaggerated the infraction and even made up a few to scare her. Taking out his handcuffs, he informed her he had to arrest her and take her back into jail. He ordered her to turn around and face the wall so he could put the cuffs on and pat her down.

- Let her determine if the sex is given or taken
- He should act stern and formal yet caring
- Include a full strip search if desired
- Creatively use handcuffs, ropes or other restraints

35 Getting Off Easy

She had worked her way very quickly through the legal system to become a judge while she was still relatively young. However her intelligence seemed to frighten off most of the men that she found attractive. Her job and various social obligations also consumed most of her time so dating was not practical. However, she found a way to use her position of power to make certain types of men eagerly service her feminine needs to the best of their abilities. Usually they wouldn't perform as well for their girlfriends, wives or mistresses but she had a way of making them focus on just her needs instead of their own. Most of the men that came through her court where there for white collar crimes. They were always dressed impeccably and gave her their utmost respect. She especially liked trying high level corporate executives and today she had a very handsome one awaiting her verdict. He was guilty but the punishment was her's to decide. She announced that she would deliberate on the sentence but first she wanted to question the defendant privately to assess his character off the record. When they were alone in her chambers, she informed him that she was willing to offer him a deal. All he had to do was pleasure her to orgasm before he got off. If he could satisfy her before himself, she would grant him a favourable judgement with a much earlier parole date. If he failed, he would be enjoying male companionship for a longer period of time.

- He should dress in a suit
- She should dress formally but without panties
- Wear a black robe if desired
- Instruct him to orally pleasure you first
- Set a time limit to give your verdict

In many ways the opposite sex is a mystery that is a source of both fascination and confusion for many people. Gender may dictate sex, but our minds have the power to determine our sexuality and how we experience sex.

Gender identity, orientation, roles, attitudes, conventions and cultural expectations all influence our sexual expression and affect our enjoyment of sex either alone or with our partner. Try adding a gender twist to a roleplay scenario - alter your normal gender roles to some degree and develop a greater empathy for your lover.

Frisky Business

Having sex at work is a very popular fantasy. The office attire, uniforms, power dynamics and day to day familiarity with each other and the working environment create a potent combination. If all the hot letters, stories and rumours about on the job hook-ups are true, there is a lot of erotic stress relief going on during working hours. After all, you do spend most of your day at work which gives you a lot of time to fantasize. Bringing your partner to work is an option but many of your coworkers or customers will obviously be potential costars in your deviant day dreams too. Although the opportunities to satisfy your desires may be hard to find in your place of work, it can be fun scheming how you could enjoy a thrilling quickie without getting caught. The forbidden, taboo nature of sex at work can make it feel even more exciting. Even if you don't expect or truly want your dirty thoughts to come true at work, these types of fantasies can be very arousing and are excellent material for sexy roleplay games with your partner in other less risky locations. But why stick with just your own occupation when you can play in all kinds of positions.

Set the Scene
- Location: bedroom, home office, closet, storage room, bathroom, garage, etc.
- Mood: pretend other people might catch you in the act
- Model the behaviour of actual coworkers or roles seen in movies
- Dress: conservative yet sexy office attire or work uniform
- Creatively use sexy accessories that might be expected in the work place

Sexy Suggestions
- Be particularly careful if you do decide to risk having sex at an actual work site especially if there are any potentially dangerous conditions in the environment
- Be aware of all the security cameras in any workplace or public location
- Having sex with your partner on a pretend managers desk can be just as rewarding and much less risky than doing it in their actual office
- Remember that fantasies of sex with coworkers does not mean you want to have a real affair and cheat on your partner
- Keep most of your clothing on during sex just in case you're about to be discovered
- Standing and rear entry positions may be best for certain scenarios

Personal Notes & Ideas

36 Naughty Staff Nurse

She worked for a large manufacturing company as the staff nurse. Since she hated seeing the men come to her with workplace injuries she was also the head of the safety committee. In fact, the policies and procedures guidelines she help bring about almost eliminated visits to her office. This was great in one way but made her job somewhat lonely and on the verge of getting boring. There were times she found herself having dirty day dreams or even surfing the web for erotic stories. She was even tempted to watch online porn a few times. All the spare time fantasizing was making her very horny. While scanning through the employee database with pictures of all the strong handsome men she used to see regularly, a wonderful idea formed in her mind. With all the noise, vibration, dust and chemicals in the work environment, random health checks with complete physicals would be a very proactive safety measure. She quickly made the pitch and received management approval with a budget to purchase anything she desired. Since many of the wives were complaining to each other about the performance of their husbands in the bedroom, she rationalized that a suite of sexual stimulation tests were just what a doctor would have ordered. She selected her first patient, called him into her office, locked the door and said with a smile "I want to assure you that every thing we do in here together is completely confidential. Let's begin by removing your shirt."

- He can dress as a construction worker or industrial machine operator
- Use various stimulation techniques (touch, smell, sight, taste, etc.) to see how he responds
- Get him to perform various sexual activities on you to test his dexterity, coordination and stamina
- Give him final instructions to have sex with his wife at least three times a week

37 Sensitivity Training

It was a sincere and genuine compliment he had given to the new secretary but apparently he had crossed the line and was now heading down to the office of internal affairs to discuss the matter. The secretary wasn't even the one who was offended - some other jealous or morally uptight employee must have overheard and reported him. He figured he would just get a stern warning and be back at his cubicle in no time. The administrative assistant told him to go in, take a seat and wait. A very hot but strict looking woman entered the office, locked the door, took a seat at her desk and opened his file. He was almost about to get himself into even more trouble when she said "You have been sent here for sensitivity training. I teach men to respect women with a rigorous program designed to improve their behaviour in as little as one session. I will assess your willingness to obey my commands and follow my rules exactly. Before we begin, let us be perfectly clear. I control whether or not you remain an employee and what kind of disciplinary action is required. You must comply immediately to all my requests and pass my tests otherwise you will be punished. Of course, you are free to go at any time. However this course of action will be understood to be your voluntary resignation." She led him into the adjoining training room and asked "Do you wish to continue?" as he surveyed what was in store for him. He was going to get more than just a 'slap on the wrist.'

- She should dress in formal business attire covering a dominatrix outfit if desired
- He should dress in a business suit, freshly shaven
- She can order him to perform various tasks then have him undress
- He can be blindfolded and made to identify items she uses to sensually stimulate him
- Use various types of BDSM equipment if desired
- Have him service her desires and then pass the final test

38 Snatch Snatch

He had been working on the ultra realistic pussy prototype for years. It had taken many long hard nights working with gorgeous models to get the perfect look and feel. Using highly sensitive sensors attached to himself and various stimulation devices, he digitally recorded all the model's vaginal characteristics through their full arousal and orgasm response cycles. Using this information combined with advances in materials and computer technology, he was able to create the ultimate artificial vagina for a line of sex robots his company was developing. His prototype could simulate how each model would react to various types and intensities of stimulation and even synthesize a full range of orgasmic reactions choreographed with other body components. He already had samples of all the other pieces assembled at a secret workshop - she just needed the most complicated module snapped into place to be a perfect pleasure system. Unfortunately, due to budget cuts, he was being escorted out of the building just as he was about to decrypt and install his software. Although he did have a backup of the software stashed away, he wasn't able to make a duplicate of the device yet for his personal pet project. He had planned for this possibility and prepared an alternate access pass to the lab so he could obtain his precious pussy and bring his carnal companion to life.

- While she lays passive on a bed, he pretends to install her pussy
- Do a systems check by performing various foreplay activities
- When turned on she performs only as directed until given the command to go into free style mode
- She can talk in a slightly robotic voice and address him as instructed
- You can switch roles with a female scientist and a penis prototype

39 Naughty Night School

When she first walked into the classroom, he was instantly attracted to her. As she wrote her name on the chalk board, he couldn't help but stare at her voluptuous ass. However it was her sexy voice and amazing accent that fueled his secret desire for her. He was there to learn a second language to get ahead in his job. Just as he was thinking it would be hard to focus on the lessons, she informed the class of her special teaching methods. She explained "Sex is a great motivator and can be used to help people learn and remember more. Since we're all adults here, I am going to help you learn how to use words in an erotic way. You'll even be able to practice using new words while seducing your partner. We will be studying various types of erotica and discover how to talk dirty even when using every day words. By using your new language with your lover, you'll naturally develop a love for the language. And, on the final day, you will be prepared to give an oral presentation based on an alluring sexual fantasy to thrill the class." Her teaching style was seductive as she enticed him to delve deep into his studies and express himself with this vibrant new language. But no matter how hard he tried, he had difficulties pronouncing certain words and phrases. On one particular night, she recommended that he stay after class so she could teach him a few special tongue exercises. Since he was prepared to go all the way, he eagerly agreed to her private lesson.

- Research some dirty, sexy sounding foreign words
- Rent a foreign language film that sounds sexy
- Practice tongue techniques on various erogenous zones then progress to her clitoris (twirls, figure eights, circles, flicks, etc.)
- Write erotic words she says with your tongue

40 Rental Agreement

He is a sleazy landlord who owns one of the better apartment buildings in the area but times are tough all over so that isn't saying much. All new tenants normally had to pass a detailed credit check however, as the owner, he sometimes made exceptions if he felt it would benefit him in the long run. When she entered his office he carefully overlooked her credit score and focused on her other more interesting attributes - young, single, sexy and financially strapped. Just as he expected, her first rent check bounced and it was almost time for her next payment. He had to pay her a visit personally and inform her about the mounting penalties he would need to impose on her if she didn't give him what he wanted. Knowing she was late with her rent, she invited him in to discuss the matter at hand and come up with a way for her to stay. Due to legal concerns he only hinted at the rent free option he had in mind. He wanted her to propose an inappropriate rental agreement involving a week by week payment plan that would make both of them happy.

- Be coy and suggestive at first
- Maybe propose an oral contract but what about the past due rent
- For more forceful play, pretend to be in the olden days when landlords may have used more overt and coercive tactics to take payment

41 Professional Pleasure Provider

As CEO she was always travelling on business so it was hard to develop or maintain a relationship. She wanted a companion for more than conversation but dating just seemed to take too much time. Until recently she hadn't even noticed or cared how much her work interfered with her love life but now she was starting to crave the intimate touch of a man. There was too much cut throat competition among her business associates so any hope of finding a good man there was out of the question. The extra office politics and gossip just wasn't worth the hassle. Feeling a little lonely in her hotel suite, she started flipping through a magazine she'd picked up at the airport and spotted an ad for male escorts. Normally the thought of paying for sex made her laugh but now she felt a quiver of naughty excitement as she entertained the idea. She hired skilled professionals in her business all the time. She even paid for exquisite spa and massage treatments so why not pay a little more to completely pamper herself and indulge in a more intense form of stress relief. With this type of rationalization she didn't give it a second thought and called the number to see if someone was available to fill an opening in her schedule.

- He should dress elegantly, be clean shaven and manicured
- Focus exclusively on her pleasure, encourage her to express all her sexual desires
- Call ahead of time to set up an appointment to build anticipation
- He can take her on a romantic date ending at a hotel
- Pretend you have a tight schedule and make an appointment for a quickie in your office during work hours
- For a more thrilling twist, pretend you're married and your secret sexual liaison is the first time you've cheated

42 Motel Room Service

As a travelling salesman, he was used to living out of a suitcase and sleeping in seedy motel rooms. Usually he would do his sales calls, get some take out and a bottle of wine then hit the sack early to be back on the road first thing in the morning usually before sunrise. Sometimes when he made a sale he would indulge in some porn then call home to his wife to enjoy a bit of phone sex with her. Since he negotiated a big contract with a nice sized commission today, that would have been his extra bonus tonight. However, his wife was at her sister's cottage for the week with no phone so, instead, it would be just some pizza, wine and a dirty movie all alone. Although the movie got him excited, something just didn't feel right and he wasn't able to get to sleep. Feeling aroused yet bored, he started flipping through a stack of flyers on the night stand. The Hot & Horny Hookups ad grabbed his attention with the promise of sexy women to service any desire. Conflicting thoughts and emotions spun around in his mind until lust finally won and he reached for the phone.

- Call girl/hooker should dress slutty with stockings, garter belt, high heels or sexy boots
- Wear a wig to feel like a different woman
- Rent a cheap motel room to make it more realistic
- Create a sexy flyer with your phone number and have him call to arrange a date

43 Arousal on Autopilot

They were strapped in and ready for take off at the end of the runway. This was a return flight with no passengers and a light crew so the stewardess doubled as a co-pilot. She was a little nervous but the captain assured her that, with his instructions, she would be able to handle the joystick like a pro. The captain encouraged her by saying "I'm going to enjoy having you in my cockpit. And, while we're flying, don't worry about going down on me. I'll be able to get it up again in no time." As the jet gained speed down the runway, the vibration and rumbling of the engines added to the thrill she experienced during lift off. She was working the joystick with a firm grip as the pilot manipulated dials and buttons to get it up in the air. When they were at cruising altitude, he let her take over in the captains chair for a while before switching to autopilot and creating their own turbulence.

- Position two padded chairs side by side as the pretend cockpit
- Play a flight simulator video game to add to the realism
- Captain can dress with a pilot hat, white shirt, dark pants, tie, pilot wings pin or badge
- Stewardess can dress in tight shirt and mini-skirt, wedge hat, scarf, gloves, no underwear
- She can use a vibrator on her chair to create the thrill of take off
- See how many flight related sexual euphemisms you can come up with while playing

44 Entry Level Position

She was in second year computer science and wanted a job in her field of study. It turned out that a neighbour owned a software company and was willing to hire her part time while she went to school. He even put her on a special project team so she could work with cutting edge technology. This was a fantasy job in more ways than one. Ever since he had moved in across the street, she had secretly watched him leave for work from her bedroom window. Many early morning masturbation sessions involved him in her erotic imagination. He was driven by his business and acted professionally whenever she was around which made her lust after him even more. At work, she would dress very conservatively on the outside while wearing sexy lingerie underneath. Early one evening he asked her to come over to his home office to help work out a problem holding up the product release. After showing her around and getting her setup, he got a call to attend an urgent client meeting. While getting changed into a suit to leave, he briefed her on the issue while she waited outside his bedroom. Instead of focusing on what he was saying, all she could think about was being in his bed. As soon as he left her alone in the house, she ran upstairs to his bed. Smelling his cologne on the pillows aroused her so much she couldn't resist stripping off her outer layer of work clothes so she could pleasure herself. Shortly after leaving, he received a call cancelling the meeting so he returned early. Hearing moans coming from his bedroom, he quietly investigated and watched her for a while before offering to help finish the job.

- He should wear a business suit and tie
- Apply a cologne she enjoys
- She can wear loose fitting clothing with a silky teddie or lacy lingerie underneath
- He can leave the house for a drive or walk to give her time to prepare
- Although shocked at being caught, he helps her relax by letting her know how he fantasized about her too

45 Scandalous Security Screening

She was going on her first vacation alone and had her bag packed ready to go. Although she wasn't expecting to meet any guys to hook up with at her destination, she was open to the possibility. Being alone to just relax and unwind would be wonderful too. Either way, she was going to enjoy herself having packed a few juicy erotic novels and a collection of her favourite sex toys. A guy or two would just add to her fun. As she walked up to the airport security, it dawned on her that all her sex toys would be visible in the x-ray scan. She blushed and started feeling nervous which made it even worse. She gave the handsome security guard an innocent smile when he looked up from the viewing monitor. When their eyes locked there was an immediate connection that made her heart race even more. He gave her a devious smile, picked up her suitcase and said "Miss, please follow me. You've been randomly selected for a more thorough check." He led her into a small windowless room, locked the door and said in a stern voice "Please stand with hands against the wall and legs spread." After slowly frisking her from head to toe, he ordered her to strip slowly as he emptied the contents of her bag onto the table. Holding her vibrator and lube, he said "I'll need you to demonstrate how these are used to ensure they're not explosive devices." After doing as she was told, she saw a huge opportunity to make him come around and give her the release she now wanted so desperately. Stroking her finger along his thigh, she pleaded "What can I do for you so you'll let me go?"

- "I need to perform a cavity search with my special equipment."
- Holding a steel butt plug, he asks "Is this some kind of weapon?"
- "You may need to make arrangements for a lay over."

46 Spin Cycle Climax

She couldn't believe the washing machine died on her again. The problem would come and go but this time she couldn't get it running no matter what she tried. Luckily she had placed a service call earlier and she was expecting the guy to show up any minute just in time to see the issue. She was hoping and praying it was still under warranty otherwise it would be a struggle to pay for it to get fixed. The repairman finally arrived and she led him in to see the machine. For some reason, the sight of him in his work uniform triggered a few erotic thoughts that made her smile. She smiled again when he bent over to put his tools on the floor in front of the machine. He tried a few standard things and of course it started working. But he took the back panel off, poked around a bit and then announced he found the problem and that he could fix it right away. While he worked, she couldn't keep her eyes off his body squirming around on the floor. When he finished, he told her he would watch it go through a complete wash cycle to confirm it worked properly. He wanted to ensure her complete satisfaction. She stood up against the machine as he filled out some paperwork. Unfortunately the washer was just out of warranty and the cost of the service call was going to be a few hundred dollars. The shock of his huge bill combined with the stimulating vibrations made her do something she could have only fantasized about before. She gave him a seductive smile, reached out to stroke between his legs and said "Is there any other way I can pay you?"

- Play while doing the laundry together
- Kiss and fondle during the wash cycle
- Time your activities to enjoy rear entry intercourse during the spin cycle with her leaning over the machine

47 Frisky Fire Fighter

Her masturbation session was cut short by an emergency call which turned out to be a false alarm. Still fully dressed in her volunteer fire fighter suit, she drove back home to continue her fantasy where she left off. On the way, she came across a man frantically waving from an open window billowing with smoke. She pulled to a stop and rushed to the house to help. The door was unlocked so she was able to get inside easily and quickly assessed the situation - he was gorgeous and half naked. He looked at her with an embarrassed smile as he pointed to his burnt dinner smoking in the sink. "I got distracted by the TV" he said just as he remembered that his porn was still playing. She glanced over at the television and smiled. Although the smoke had cleared, he looked like he still needed her assistance desperately and she knew just what to do.

- "You look hungry. I'm already hot, juicy and ready to eat."
- "You're doing a great job", "I've had years of practice going down on the pole."
- "How about you put your wood in my fire?"
- Female fire fighter costume - authentic or sexy version

48 Snip and a Shave

They had discussed it for months. He finally gave in when she threatened to cut them off herself or stop having sex with him. It would just be a little snip and then condom free sex for the rest of his life. But even that thought didn't ease his mind as he laid on the table waiting. His wife was in the waiting room so he couldn't just make a run for it. Just before he lost his nerve, an extremely gorgeous nurse came into the room and peaked under his gown. With a very sexy voice she said "I need to do some prep work on you before the doctor can see you." She plugged in the hair clippers and removed his gown. She flashed him a sweet smile when she saw his erection and got down to business trimming his bush. He blushed with embarrassment but with the tingly vibrations of the clipper it got even harder. She then applied shaving cream all over making sure to massage it in. After delicately shaving him completely smooth, she wiped him clean and said "Now it looks bigger too." He looked down to admire her work and noticed she was applying lube to her finger. "What's that for?" he asked with a slight quiver in his voice. She looked him in the eyes and lied "We need you to fully unload" as she inserted her finger where he least expected it. "And we don't want to make another mess so ..." She lowered her head to take him in her mouth.

- Wear a sexy nurse uniform or dress in a white shirt, skirt and nylons
- Use latex gloves and your finger, butt plug, anal dildo or prostate massager with lots of lube to stimulate an intense orgasm
- She can get on the table (bed) in a 69 position to help 'distract' him while she's performing her job
- Schedule a followup appointment to perform some more extensive tests and to obtain a sample

49 Opening to Close

When she first showed him the house, he was discreet but she could tell from his eyes that he wanted her. As an attractive realtor, she did like to flaunt her sex appeal to help make the deal. However with this guy, she could feel his eyes undressing her. For some reason she sensed he was imagining having sex with her in various positions in each and every room of the house. This made her think along the same lines which secretly aroused her. It took all her effort to keep her composure. He was definitely interested and arranged a second more private showing to do an intimate inspection before making an offer. This time he was more forward but with carefully chosen words that were clean and appropriate yet extremely suggestive. At least in her mind, he was hinting for her to sweeten the deal and she was starting to fall for his charm. However he left her with only a handshake that sent shivers through her body. She rushed home to relieve the mounting tension she had built up during the encounter. The next day the lawyers received the unconditional offer at the full asking price which was immediately accepted by the owner. She just needed to get the buyer to sign the final draft. He wanted her to bring the papers over to the house and give him one last tour through each room before he signed. She knew that this time she would need to satisfy his final demands to get her big commission.

- He should dress stylish and elegant
- She should dress in a sexy business outfit with high heels and stockings
- Pretend you are having sex in another person's home
- Pretend she is married and requires more pressure to open herself to temptation
- Put on a new bedspread or have sex in a different room

50 Sperm Bank Deposit

It was his first time coming here so he felt a little nervous. The receptionist took one look at him and knew he was going to need some help to over come his inhibitions. Even though it looked like he had been saving it up for quite a while, it was going to take some special handling to get a good sample to come out. She walked over to one of the unoccupied rooms, motioned to him and said "Come in here." She handed him a clipboard with a standard information form and semen utilization agreement. "Just wait here and relax, our nurse will be coming shortly." When the nurse came, the way she looked in her sexy uniform made him spring to attention. She took the clipboard from him and said "Please come and sit down next to me while we go over your sexual history together." After asking him a serious of questions, she said "We're coming to the end. We want to know about your sexual fantasies and what turns you on so we can prepare for when you come again. As you're telling me, strip off all your cloths and then I'll come to give you a full examination before we start." As she intimately touched and stroked his body from head to toe, she informed him "I'll do whatever it takes to help you come for me." When they were done and he was about to leave, the receptionist paid him and said "Thank You, Please come again soon."

- Be sure to have him ejaculate into a small sample container
- "We need to flush out your system to get fresh sperm. I'll take your first sample and save the second in this container."
- The nurse encourages him to fondle her and perform oral sex on her while getting him ready for his second coming
- Use anal sex toys or a gloved finger with lube to massage his prostate if desired

Whether it's making love in an exotic location or having sex in a fantasy scenario, the setting makes it special. Certain details will trigger thoughts and emotions that magnify physical sensations to make sex exceptionally wonderful.

Using a little creativity, a variety of props and a few elements of scenery, you can fulfill a dream or fantasy in your own home. Design and create a special setting that allows you to be carried away on an erotic adventure. Combined with your imagination, it can seem more real than being there.

Maids, Masters & Mistresses

The classic French and English maid uniforms are viewed by many people (both men and women) to be very sexy. Various types of maid style outfits (uniforms, costumes, lingerie) are popular for use in and out of the bedroom. The seductive outfit contrasts with the demure and submissive behaviour expected of a maid. Combine this with the wealth, power and absolute authority commanded by the master or mistress of the house and you have a scenario dripping with erotic possibilities. The prim and proper facade only adds to the sexual tension. Secret romantic trysts, illicit affairs and coerced sexual services can all play out in an atmosphere of elegance. The lady of the house can also indulge her desires with any of the available man servants or play with the maids if she prefers.

Set the Scene
- Location: master bedroom, spare bedroom, den, hotel
- Emphasize the dominant and obedient roles
- Servant: wear a sexy maid or butler outfit
- Black and white uniform, high heels, stockings
- Master: dress and act as a stern authority figure
- Mistress: governess style dress or nightgown
- Feather duster, serving tray, drinks

Sexy Suggestions
- Spankings as punishment for improper performance
- Have sex with most of the maid outfit still on
- Make up your own look for a sexy man servant to service the mistress
- A bath is a perfect place to be pampered and pleasured
- Enjoy sex with the warm glow of a fireplace

Personal Notes & Ideas

51 Bed Turn Down Service

It was a long, tough day of contract negotiations and he was looking forward to getting back to his hotel suite to unwind. A stiff drink, some time to relax and a good night sleep would be a perfect way to top off the day. After taking a shower to freshen up before going to sleep, he noticed the luxurious looking bed wasn't turned down yet. Although he wasn't too upset, the management of this prestigious hotel insisted that he notify them of any detail they may have overlooked. They even promised to compensate extra for any deficiency found in their service. A few minutes after informing the front desk, there was a knock on his door. He answered it to find a young lady dressed in a very sexy French maid outfit pushing a service trolley with an assortment of delicious treats. She apologized for the bed and then said "I'm here to attend to your every desire until you're ready to go to sleep. I will do anything to help you have the most wonderful night ever." He couldn't help getting turned on as he watched her walk to bed and turn it down. Feeling his eyes focused on her, she bent over to give him an even better view. She smiled coyly as she noticed his growing interest and knew he was going to give her a big tip for the excellent bedroom service he was about to receive.

- Make up your bed with fresh sheets
- Prepare a tray of chocolates and fruit
- Serve him a drink and a few appetizers
- Offer a neck massage leading to more sensual pleasures
- He can dress as a butler or French maid to service a female client

52 Maid to Spy

Being in the country illegally, she was always on guard and tried to stay under the radar but they eventually found her. However, rather than deporting her, they made her an offer she couldn't refuse. Apparently she had certain assets and skills that would come in handy for a certain under cover job they had in mind for her. The secret service was investigating a mob boss with international political ties and she just happened to be one of his maids. The plan was simple. All she had to do was keep him occupied long enough for another agent to sneak into his home office. They didn't tell her what they were doing or looking for, only that she needed to keep him occupied for at least an hour. How she accomplished that task was completely up to her.

- Dress as a sexy maid with stockings, garters and high heels
- Find him in any room other than his office
- Ask if he wants a drink and if he minds her finishing her work
- Give him an erotic show while dusting and attempting to seduce him

53 Victorian Maid

The master of the house was known to be a stern and disciplined gentleman who demanded strict obedience to his authority. There were rumours that his prudish and moral behaviour was just a facade hiding a lecherous beast whose deviant desires were only unleashed behind closed doors. Although she dismissed these tales as slanderous gossip, she secretly fantasized about being forced to submit to perverse acts of pleasure. While appearing shy and innocent herself, she craved someone who could release the wild sexual urges pent up in her mind and body. When she was hired, she felt a mixture of lust and fear for her new employer. But after a month of demanding service, her needs were left unsatisfied. With increasing frustration bordering on hysteria, she accidentally knocked over an expensive glass vase. Hearing the crash, he ordered her into his den. Terrified of losing her job or worse, she entered the room with her head lowered awaiting his wrath. He closed the door behind her and calmly said "You are now indebted to me. I've been watching you and I know just how you can repay me. But first, you need to be punished."

- Bending over his knee, she receives a spanking that makes her hot and wet
- As she wiggles against his leg begging for mercy, they both get aroused
- With increasing lust he then takes more liberties with her body
- Before allowing her an orgasm he orders her to pleasure him

54 Bedding the Butler

She was married to a rich and powerful man and lived a life of luxury. Although outwardly prim and proper, she longed for the physical pleasures described in the many erotic books she had discovered in her husband's study. He did have sex with her once a month to fulfill his duties but never with any passion or excitement. Since his work consumed all his attention, she was usually left alone with the maid servants, her butler and her husband's books. As she read more, her desires increased and she started to fantasize about her butler and even the maids. She attempted to flirt and seduce him but he fought hard to resisted her advances. This made it even more fun and encouraged her to try more suggestive and enticing tactics to arouse his interest. Finally, one night when her husband was away on business, she dressed in her finest lingerie and called her butler to her bedside. She requested that he make a drink for both of them, then handed him a book and said "Please read this story to me."

- Pretend to be in a Victorian, old South or modern era mansion
- While the butler reads, she slowly and sensually fondles herself
- He resists her temptation as long as possible
- She can either beg or demand that he pleasure her

55 Masturbating Maid Even More Fun

He was the only heir of an aristocratic family returning home from military school. When he arrived, she caught his eye but made sure she stayed away from him while his parents were around. They hadn't seen each other in years but she fondly remembered the times they secretly played together growing up. And, although relations with the servants was strictly forbidden, he dreamed of her every night he was away. As a young teenager, she had shown him a secret passage to the maid's quarters where he could watch them undressing, bathing and playing with each other naked. She would tease him by kissing and intimately touching the other girls. When no one else was around, they would explore each other's bodies and dream of being together in a far off land. The fear of being caught made their time together even more exciting. Now that he was a virile young man and she was a voluptuous young woman, they could hardly resist the temptation to rush into each other's arms. Finally, as everyone turned in for the night, he snuck down to her room where he knew she was expecting him. With a single candle illuminating her bed, he watched as she slowly teased herself for his pleasure and hers. Even though it had been such a long time away from her, he was more than happy to enjoy her show before joining her on the bed.

- Make love as slowly and quietly as possible to avoid being caught
- Choose positions and activities that create less noise
- Periodically stop to listen for any one approaching or watching

56 Customer Appreciation Night

He met her at a very nice restaurant to discuss his employment with her escort agency. She had a very exclusive client list and demanded the best companions for the wealthy women willing to indulge in her services. Her background checks on him were very extensive. Although references in this business were hard to come by, he was able to provide her with testimonials from a few of his own clients. She was impressed by his charm and sophistication but wasn't shy about grilling him on his sexual knowledge and skills. Rather than testing him herself, she had arranged for one of her best customers to give him a more intimate evaluation. This lady had an appreciation for the qualities of a great gigolo and a deep empathy for the needs and desires of their clients. The men who measured up to her standards all scored exceptionally well with the other members. A free session in recognition of her loyal business and grading expertise would help all three of them. She handed him the details of his trial date night on the back of a specially embossed business card which also identified him as her employee. After receiving the customer review of his service during the night, she would let him know if more business would be sent his way or not. With a smile she wished him good luck and left him to plan for the evening.

- Meet for lunch in a restaurant to give him the date details
- Make plans for a special evening out with opportunities for romance
- Dress more elegant than normal
- Arrange a hotel room if desired
- He should focus on pleasuring her completely
- Research a few new sensual techniques to try (erotic massage, cunnilingus, exotic sex positions, etc.)

Erotic Photography

Almost every couple has a digital camera of some sort available to take a few hot shots of each other in deliciously provocative poses. There are also many software tools to edit and touch up the photos to turn them into works of art. Many people really enjoy either taking photos or being the center of attention in the pictures. And, since you no longer need to send film out to be developed, your digital pictures can be as risqué and explicit as you desire. You can make them glamorous, sexy, kinky or even downright dirty and nasty. You can also take as many as you want during the photo session then delete all but a select few exceptional shots. The erotic photographer's job is to help the subject get comfortable and encourage them to make love to the camera so they can capture truly amazing images. As if seducing the model with compliments, they continually describe the beautiful, alluring and aesthetically pleasing qualities focused through their lens. As the model gets into the flow of posing, they willingly follow instructions to become increasingly provocative for the camera and ultimately the photographer. It's easy for the photographer to be seduced by this power and take advantage of the model's almost submissive desire to please.

Set the Scene
- Location: studio, living room or bedroom
- Clean and tidy the 'studio' and even rearrange some furniture if desired
- Her Dress: semi formal dress or business attire with sexy under garments
- Full make up and hair styling
- Use one or more real cameras with additional photography equipment if available (lights, flash, tri-pod, etc.)
- Assortment of different styles of lingerie (bras, panties, teddies, silky, lacy, etc.)
- Purchase some unique styles of clothing you wouldn't normally wear at a thrift shop
- Elegant throw pillows, silk scarves, feather, costume jewelry and other erotic accoutrements
- Variety of sex toys if desired for more explicit shots

Sexy Suggestions
- Use lots of sincere compliments describing in detail what you love about the sexy vision in your sights
- Focus on specific details that turn you on and how you want the model to accentuate them

Personal Notes & Ideas

57 Lingerie Model

The publishing company called him with a fantastic opportunity to create a new online magazine focused on lingerie. They even sent a box of samples to use in his initial design concepts. He was also given a small budget to purchase new items and accessories to accentuate the look of his special models. He knew the perfect girl to model the style of lingerie that he had in mind. He called her to see if she was interested in the lingerie modelling project. As he expected, she was so excited and eager to get started, she came immediately.

- Go out shopping together to purchase a few new items of lingerie for her to model
- Pick out one or two pieces of sexy male evening wear so you can both get in the pictures
- Start with her lounging in lingerie on a sofa or love seat then move to the bedroom 'studio'
- Explore shots with partial nudity then decide on the fly how edgy or hardcore you both want to go

58 Perfect Head Shot

She desperately wanted to get into modelling and eventually work her way into acting. To get started, she needed to get a few really good head shots to send out to various agencies. Her friend who was already in the business gave her the name of a guy she used for her head shots. He was considered one of the best in the business and had the connections to get her into some high profile modelling positions if he liked her that is. She called and arranged an appointment. He recommended she get herself completely dolled up as if she were going out to an elegant, formal event. A manicure and nail polish was also important since her hands might be in the shot. Just before she went to his studio, her friend checked her out and said "You look absolutely gorgeous. He's going to love you. Remember, just do everything he tells you without question." Then, with a sly smile, she added "I know you'll give him the best head he's ever had in his studio."

- Take some 'normal' head shots commenting on her alluring eyes and luscious lips
- "You look perfect for a number of high profile magazine features my clients are working on."
- "We need a few seductive and sexy pictures that reveal more of what you have to offer."
- "To help get you the most amazing jobs possible, I need some close up shots of you giving me your best head."
- While he's taking pictures of you giving him a blow job, make sure to look into the camera at times and let him see how much you enjoy making him shoot

59 Passionate Boudoir Photo Session

She was a stereotypical bored housewife who just wanted to feel sexy again. The daily monotony was draining her energy and enthusiasm and lately it wasn't being properly replenished in the bedroom either. She desperately wanted to reignite the passion and excitement in her marriage. As a pick me up for herself and hopefully her sex life too, she decided to get a boudoir portrait done. She planned to give it to her husband as a surprise on their anniversary so she arranged an in home photo session while he was on a business trip. The photographer was renowned for bringing out the seductive charm and alluring beauty that every woman possessed. His portraits were considered works of sensual erotic art that captured the fiery passion of the women he photographed. His clients raved that their portraits conveyed the essence of their secret desires and stimulated hot, lustful, almost jealous arousal in their partners. Apparently, he was able to unleash their inner sex goddess and capture proof that she was still alive and well. She couldn't wait for him to come.

- Encourage her to dress in a way that she identifies with sexually and feels most attractive
- While snapping pictures in different poses, give her sexy compliments and turn her on with dirty talk
- Stimulate her desire and instruct her to build her arousal using fantasy, fingers and toys
- Feed her craving for loving attention and then fill her need with what she wants most

60 Private Penis Portfolio

She was a photographer who specialized in doing celebrity glamour shots for magazines and online promotions. She was particularly fond of doing men because of a side hobby she enjoyed for her own personal pleasure. Similar to the 'plaster caster', she had her own way of capturing memories of the stars she worked on. Not all of them agreed to reveal their magnificent manhood but she had ways to encourage almost every man to give in to her artistic desires. From her early days in the high school photography club until now, she had amassed an impressive portfolio of penises in all shapes and sizes. With artistic style, she captured erections as erotic masterpieces suitable for framing. Most of her clients usually wanted a print for themselves. Word of mouth was making her business and her hobby spring to life. And today she's eagerly looking forward to see a special new client rumoured to be exceptionally well endowed.

- He should dress as a movie, sports or music star ready for a magazine cover shot
- Start by taking regular photos in various poses complimenting him on his physique
- Encourage him to slowly start to reveal more of his body
- Do what ever it takes to get permission to include him in your private collection
- He may need her special skills to help make him rise for the occasion

61 Wrinkled Wedding Gown

He was a renowned wedding photographer with a reputation for making brides extremely happy. All the brides in his pictures had a gleam in their eyes, a serene smile and a glow of happiness about them. His skill involved creating an intimate connection with the women he photographed so they felt more comfortable with him and his camera. With almost hypnotic affect, he could seduce them and redirect their nervous energy into passionate desire and arousal. His suggestive instructions encouraged them to make love to the camera with a mixture of innocence and lust. Of course, he could only do this kind of work in private with his subject so he created his own mobile studio to perform his magic at the wedding site. He could capture the bride's beauty just before she rushed to the alter. Today, the bride seems to have cold feet so he needs to do something extra special to warm her up for the wedding otherwise he's not going to get paid.

- Dress in a full wedding gown or all white lingerie with cream stockings, pearl choker, garters, veil, etc.
- An orgasm should help relieve her jitters but does she need a soft warm tongue or a hard hot cock to make her pussy melt for marriage
- Perform oral sex under her gown and enjoy intercourse standing up while fully dressed even if it means the wedding gown may get wrinkled
- Pretend you have an anxious crowd of people waiting outside for you to finish

Although you may not be into any special type of kinky sex or fetish, there is nothing that says you can't experiment to see what all the fuss is about. Even if they don't arouse you, the potential fun factor may be exhilarating.

Sexual kinks or fetishes include: bondage, leather, rubber, piercing, costumes, golden showers, food, feet, spanking, etc. Do some research together with your partner to discover potential sexual kinks, fetishes or special erotic accessories that you would be willing to explore to spice up your sex play.

Staged Sex Scenes

With advances in technology, high quality digital video cameras have become very affordable. Even cheap web cameras and most cell phones are now able to record good quality video. Most modern computers also come with free or inexpensive video editing software with easy to use special effects. With these tools almost anyone can create professional looking movies. If you identify as a voyeur, director or star, you'll love making your own dirty movies to add more sizzle to your love life. The objective is to have fun and then see yourselves enjoying each other from a different point of view later. Even pretending to be on camera can be an exhilarating experience. Or just watch the good parts then delete the footage. Either way, get out your video camera, pick a passionate plot and get ready to say "Action!"

Set the Scene
- Location: variable depending on the desired plot and scene
- Use props, accessories, costumes to make the scene more realistic
- Write a brief script with basic action sequences and sample dialog
- Campy porn producer dressed sleazy with open shirt, chains, sun glasses
- One or more digital video cameras (hand held and on tripod)
- Lingerie and skimpy clothing (tight shorts and t-shirts, bikinis, etc.)
- Glamorous or retro style outfits obtained from a thrift store
- A variety of sex toys with water based lube

Sexy Suggestions
- You may feel nervous with stage fright the first few times so encourage each other to giggle, laugh out loud and break character whenever you need to then continue playing
- Wearing a sexy mask to hide your identity may help you get into character more easily
- Enjoy the foreplay and sexual pleasure you're having together rather than trying to create a performance
- Penises can get stage fright too but will come around if you focus on the pleasures of kissing, stroking and licking each other
- Forget the 'money shot' if it means sacrificing her orgasm to get it
- Use ice cubes to get pert nipples for erotic close up shots
- Do some test shots ahead of time to check the lighting and practice using the equipment so you can focus on the fun
- Keep the cameras rolling to capture everything then edit together all the good bits later if you desire

Personal Notes & Ideas

62 Sex In The Spotlight

Tuition for the final year of their theatrical studies course was looming in their mind when they came across a flyer for an acting contest at a local night club. Reading closer they discovered it was an erotically themed event intended to include live sex as part of the show. Although a little hesitant at first, the $10,000 grand prize sealed the deal for both of them. They quickly worked out a script, designed some costumes and obtained a few props to include in their show. It would start with an erotic dance to build desire, passion and excitement. While dancing, suggestive fondling and kissing would lead to a strip tease for their audience. Then they would tantalize the crowd with a number of different foreplay activities before having sex in a variety of positions. A dramatic climax would close their show hopefully to a standing ovation and a number one finish. Their act left room for plenty of improv opportunities to arouse the crowd and each other. After many intense rehearsals, tonight would be their debut erotic performance. The crowd began cheering as the music started, the house lights dimmed and the spot light focused on the stage ready for a thrilling live sex show.

- Prepare a stage in the middle of a large room
- Create a playlist of music with cheering crowd sound effects added between songs
- Use a spotlight or a few flashlights in a dark room
- Dress in any costume with glitter makeup or body paints if desired
- Include props for visual effect and to help with creative sex positions (exercise ball, chair, pillows, sex toys, etc.)
- Imagine you are demonstrating your sexual skills to raving fans in the audience and they are encouraging you to show even more wild moves

63 Wicked Wife Wants to Watch

It was another late night at the office but he was finally home looking forward to a drink and some quiet time alone. Since his wife was out of town on business, the guys had wanted him to go out to a few strip joints with them. He was definitely tempted but had promised to do a web chat with his wife later that night. She had suggested the virtual date might lead to some cyber sex as an appetizer for when she got back home. It sounded like fun so he wasn't going to blow that off especially when he could do the strippers the following night. When he opened the door, he immediately sensed something was strange. He cautiously looked around and noticed a chair in the middle of the living room with a computer on a small table set off to the side. All the other furniture was pushed against the walls. The computer had a screen saver with a message bouncing around as it displayed pictures of a model doing a strip tease. His mind raced as he read the message "Click, Sit and Watch" but he did as instructed. He was only partially relieved when the screen flashed to show his wife on the web cam. Before he could speak, she said "Sit down. We Don't Need to Talk". Just then, the lights dimmed and some soft sensual music started to play. A very exotic stripper slowly revealed herself.

- Create a playlist of music you enjoy dancing to
- Slowly remove your clothing to build anticipation
- Apply a new perfume to various areas of your body
- Enforce a no touching rule until after your lap dance
- Have sex using the chair in creative positions
- Slow dance together naked afterwards

64 Casting Couch

He was an unscrupulous porn producer looking for new talent to exploit for his personal pleasure and profit. His ads in the help wanted section of the local newspaper never failed to lure in gorgeous women looking to make some quick easy money. One or two girls would definitely make the cut to be an adult video star and make his investment worth the effort. However, what he enjoyed the most was giving each girl a thorough private audition and a chance to prove how good she was and just how much she was willing to do for a job. He took great satisfaction seeing how far he could get each girl to go making a demo video with him as her co-star, camera man and director. The interview would start out normal enough with him giving an overview of the opportunities in the industry and then asking some questions about her background. This included her sexual history and the type of scenes she would be willing to perform in. If she was still interested, he would encourage her to slowly and sensually reveal her assets for the camera until she was completely naked. After filming every detail of her body in various erotic poses, he would get her to masturbate for the camera. With shameless praise of her porn star qualities, he would eventually direct her to orally pleasure him while he filmed her in close up detail. Depending on his mood, intercourse in various positions and even anal sex would then be followed by a glorious money shot or "cream pie" segment.

- Play in an office, den or living room with a couch
- Use a handheld video camera to record the audition
- He needs to "test" her acting abilities performing and taking direction in front of a camera
- Have her demonstrate how she would play with a variety of different sex toys to pleasure both herself and the many viewers
- He can entice her to hold the camera while he orally pleasures her
- Switch roles with a female producer looking for male talent

65 Recording The Message

They were a very close knit group of girl friends even though they had moved to different parts of the country to pursue individual careers. Ever since high school, they had always dared each other to try new and outrageous things. Considering their frisky and naughty nature, sex was usually involved in some creative way. Each of them had to do the task in turn while the others secretly watched. When she saw the email with the title "Dare: Record the Message", she knew something new and exciting was about to happen. Apparently sometime that night she would be contacted with a special message. It was her job to do everything possible to ensure the entire message was revealed while recording the encounter with concealed video cameras. All her friends would also be watching online via her webcam. She knew that part of the message would be in their private code and it would indicate what else she was expected to do. She had everything setup just as the doorbell rang. When she opened the door, she couldn't help turning to the cameras and giving her friends a big smile. Although his costume was realistic enough, she could tell right away that he was there to deliver a strip-o-gram. It was her job to act surprised, demonstrate her arousal, encourage him to strip completely and then ravish him. Depending upon various words in his message, she may need to fake an orgasm, strip herself, masturbate, orally pleasure him or perform any number of other deliciously dirty deeds.

- Prepare some music to dance/strip to
- He can prepare a few love notes to sing as part of the show or just use the song lyrics as the message
- He can wear a special costume (officer, fireman, clown, cowboy, construction worker, etc.) if desired
- He should dance seductively before allowing her to touch
- Officially he's not "allowed" to remove his g-string or have sex with the customer so she'll need to entice him

66 Sex Appeal Sells

She was an up and coming actress looking to get any kind of exposure and was willing to do almost anything to get ahead in the industry. When her agent called to tell her about a sexy marketing job modelling for commercials, she couldn't wait to start. He informed her that she would be doing product demonstrations that would be made into advertisements for DVD and web promotions with world wide distribution. In addition to great pay and experience working with a well known director, she would even get royalties on the product sales. Trusting her agent, she signed the contract without reading it. For the first assignment there would be no script. The director wanted to capture her initial reaction to the products and record how she used them. When she arrived at the studio, they whisked her into makeup for a complete make over including a new hair style, manicure and pedicure. She was then given some very sexy lingerie and a silk robe to put on before being led to the director who was already on set. Little did she realize that she had come to shoot with sex toys.

- Buy a new sex toy as a surprise for her to unwrap on the bed
- Use this as a good reason to get dolled up for sex
- Record her initial reaction to the product then encourage her to play with it
- She can play either shy at first (needing to be reminded of her contract) or be excited, eager and uninhibited
- While the video cameras are rolling, take some still shots as you compliment her work
- Send in a co-star to help demonstrate the product if desired

Sex can seem more fun and exciting when it involves something that is naughty, outrageous or even a bit scandalous. Fear of being exposed or caught can heighten the sexual intensity.

*Consider semi-public sex, affairs with your spouse, cross dressing, partner swapping, attending a sex party, etc. Even discussing your naughty desires with your lover can be arousing. How can you make your sex play **feel** more outrageous and scandalous without the risks?*

Like a Virgin

Virginity is often associated with someone young and innocent but it can also be about someone who is sexually curious, seductive or naughty. There is a mystique associated with taking someone's virginity that can be very intense and emotional. A woman's virginity is highly valued in many cultures today as it was throughout history – a prize to be rewarded, taken or even sacrificed and which must be guarded carefully. But even male virginity is often prized by women. What ever your beliefs, you can recreate your first time again and pretend you are a virgin with your current partner or even enjoy an erotic "deflowering" fantasy together. If you desire, you can rewrite your sexual history and recapture (or create) the exciting thrill of first time sex over and over again.

Set the Scene
- Location: car, living room, bedroom, motel room
- Pigtails, ponytail, braids or curls create a youthful look
- Bows, ribbons, ankle or knee high socks, sneakers, lollipop
- Virginity is usually associated with sweet, pure, inexperienced innocence
- Pretend to be naive, shy, nervous and even a little frightened yet eager and excited too

Sexy Suggestions
- As mental foreplay, go out shopping together to find special clothing that makes you feel younger or more innocent
- Virgin roleplay during your period adds to the visual realism and an orgasm helps with cramps too
- Use dark sheets with a white towel or cloth if you want the visual effect with real or fake blood
- Work in your own creative male or female "proof of virginity" tests if you wish
- Substitute anal sex for regular intercourse

Personal Notes & Ideas

67 Deflowering Plot

He's the gardener and maintenance man at a private all girls school. Other than the very stern head master, he's the only other guy allowed on the premises. Since the girls tend to the grounds work as part of their learning duties, he only needed to come by once or twice a week to do the heavy labour or to fix something. It gave him a thrill catching the girls secretly staring at him from a distance. However, he could never imagine the sexual fantasies inspired by his presence. Little did he know that a small group of girls devised a plan to make theirs come true. They weren't content learning about the birds and bees from books. They wanted hands on experience to complete their sex education and planned for him to give it to them in the utility shed. The small building would give them the privacy they needed and it even had a cot for overnight stays. It was off limits to all the girls but that made their plan even more exciting. At the end of the day when he goes to put away his tools and get ready to leave, he's surprised to see four young women waiting for him. They entice him with their budding breasts and the delicate petals between their legs then offer their chosen one to be deflowered professionally.

- Wear a girls school uniform and slowly strip to entice him to show his equipment
- Encourage him to touch you and react as though it's a new and intense sensation
- Pretend that seeing, touching and sucking a penis is a totally new experience
- Pretend you are the one to be deflowered while the three other girls watch or make out together
- Play some girl on girl porn in the background to set the mood if desired

68 Late for the Reception

It had been a long wait getting all the arrangements organized but they were finally married. After reciting their vows to each other, they exchanged their wedding rings and kissed each other passionately. It was a wonderful morning ceremony at a scenic church. There was lots of time before the reception for guests to mingle and take pictures. But, for the bride and groom, this extra time was planned because they had something very important to do before partying all night. Through a shower of confetti, they rushed to their limo and sped off toward the hotel. They couldn't keep their hands off each other in the back seat. While most other couples these days had sex before marriage, they had waited and it was desperately hard. Today, as planned, they were on their way to consummate their marriage while they were still fresh and sober. It would give them even more to celebrate later.

- For added realism rent a hotel room and show up fully dressed as a bride and groom
- Share some champagne as you make love slowly and sensually building up for the 'first time'
- Make love while still wearing some wedding clothes (stockings, garter, pearl choker, hair piece)

69 Dungeon Bait

At the palace ball the princess was mesmerizing. She had come of age and was using her seductive charms to flirt with all the attractive noblemen while ignoring the eligible suitors invited by her parents. More interested in having some fun, she relished the fear she caused with her alluring attention. Everyone knew the royal decree protecting her purity and the severe punishment for any man caught alone with her. Sensing her awakening desires, the king and queen had become extra vigilant of guarding her virginity until she was married off to a suitable prince. However, one man fearlessly met her enticing gaze and didn't shy away from her playful advances. While dancing together, she slipped a key and a note into his pocket. Then, quickly whispering in his ear, she informed him that it would unlock her chastity belt. With a flourishing twirled, she left to tease someone else and draw attention away from him so he could read the note privately. It contained instructions for a secret way into her bedroom and a dare to use the key after midnight.

- Dress up as a princess complete with tiara
- Design your own chastity belt to be unlocked
- Be as quiet as you can having sex to avoid getting caught by the guards or the king

70 King Takes Wedding Night

The country is ruled by a tyrannical king who longs for a queen to rule by his side. Although he has the power to take anything he wants, there are no suitable princess brides available. Emissaries returned from the furthest known kingdoms with news that all royal virgins of age had been married off. In a fit of rage he vowed that he would find a queen in his own kingdom even if he had to deflower every virgin peasant or nobel woman in the land. And, to ensure no other man could take a wife that might be the queen he desired, he decreed that every bride had to spend their wedding night with him first. The marriage would not become official until after he made his assessment of her worthiness to be his queen. The evaluation included sex. If she was the one, they would be married immediately. If she wasn't, he would take his pleasure and release her. But if any failed his virginity test, they would be executed. Tonight, royal guards have taken you from your wedding ceremony and escorted you to the king's bedroom. Will you be the new queen?

- Be fearfully subservient to king and indulge every whim
- The king may undress and intimately inspect you
- Be sexually innocent but willing to comply for the king's pleasure

71 The Waiting is Over

You are both virgins, the wedding is finally over and so is the waiting. You have exchanged your purity rings for wedding rings and now you are both alone in the hotel room as husband and wife. The hard days of abstinence are over. To guard against temptation, you haven't even seen each other naked before. Everything is going to be completely new but you want to take it slow and enjoy every nuance of this new experience with the person you absolutely love and adore. To make it special and loving, you tentatively touch, kiss and gently caress each other as you focus on each new luscious sensation. You know you have all night to explore each other intimately for the very first time so you want it to last.

- Rent a hotel room or quickly redecorate your bedroom (fresh sheets, flowers, extra throw pillows, etc.)
- Get a bottle of champagne, strawberries, oysters and chocolates
- Go all out with a white wedding dress and suit/tuxedo or skip right to some white lingerie and silk boxers
- Put on some romantic music and dance sensually as you undress each other slowly
- Make love while still wearing some of your wedding clothes
- Look deeply into each other's eyes as you tenderly initiate intercourse for the first time

72 Prom Night Nookie

Dressed up and dancing close to each other all night is driving you both crazy with anticipation. You've planned this for months and have both been saving yourselves for this special occasion. The night is going to be perfect – limo service, a few drinks, the motel room and a late curfew. You both look amazing, you've graduated and there's only one thing to take care of before you can truly consider yourself adults.

- Dress up as though you are going to a real prom dance (or roleplay teenagers if you are going to an actual dance)
- Pretend you are virgin high school graduates
- Prolong the anticipation by slow dancing together for a number of songs while kissing and surreptitiously fondling each other (remember the chaperones are watching)
- Sneak a few drinks while you are dancing to add a feeling of being naughty
- When you are finally in a private bedroom, slowly undress each other while you continue to dance
- Slow dance together naked before letting your passions run wild

73 Hymen Trophy

You're the sexy cheer leader, he's the school sports star and you've just won the championship. To top it off, he's been voted the most outstanding player demonstrating a dedication to excellence and integrity. He's also received a scholarship to the same college you've been accepted to and you have decided to share a dorm room together. So now is as good a time as any to celebrate and lose your virginity at the same time. There's a big house party planned and you've arranged to have one of the bedrooms reserved for just the two of you. Only question is – do you make out in your uniforms or not? Either way, you are going to give him a very special trophy that you will both remember for the rest of your lives. Like a good cheer leader, you know exactly how to motivate him to win big and he's not one to come up short.

- Dress in a cheer leader outfit with pom-poms
- Prepare a fun erotic cheer to get in the mood
- He can wear a favourite sport team's jersey or gear
- He can do some pre-play exercise to work up a sweat if she enjoys the smell of a man fresh from a workout

74 High School Sweet Hearts

You are teenagers in love. The first kiss, holding hands, necking, cuddling and fondling have made your pulses race but you haven't gone all the way yet. That is until tonight! While inexperienced, you're both horny, eager and ready for more. One way or another, you're going to find a way to have sex for the first time. The only question is when and where are you going to be able to do it. Can you encourage your parents to go out and leave you alone for a few hours? Can you borrow a car and make out in the back seat? Is there a safe and secret hiding place at school? Maybe he can sneak into your room at night? He would need to crawl through your window and keep very quiet so your parents won't hear you. Or should you skip school and run off to a secluded spot in the middle of the day?

- Dress in clothing reminiscent of your youth or in a sexy style worn by teenagers today
- Put on a younger style of make-up (cherry lip gloss, flashy nail polish, etc.)
- As mental foreplay, go for a coffee date and plan a secret liaison for later - work out all the details to ensure you won't get caught
- Come up with a list of various possible locations to lose your virginity then try out all the different variations on special anniversaries

75 Late Bloomer Deflowered

She's the lead biologist working on a government research program cataloging the properties of flowers, their pollen and seeds. You are her lab assistant working close by her side for the past few months. She's prim and proper on the outside but you know she's ready to burst with sexual desire. During your daily discussions, she described her single minded career focus and how hard she worked to get her PhD. She also informed you how she studiously excluded all men from her life and even confided that she was still a virgin. Now that her career goals have been met, you sense her female needs are starting to flower. You see her beauty even though she tries to hide it. She's afraid of her lust but secretly craves all the young men that pass her by and that includes you. It's time to use your charms to crack her cold exterior and release her inhibitions. Show her how to "let her hair down" and prepare yourself for the most wildly intense sex of your life.

- She pretends to be a mature virgin
- Dress in a lab coat or conservative business attire
- Seduce her in the lab, her office, arrange a "working" dinner or show up late with lab results and a bottle of wine

76 Orgasmic Ritual Offering

You are the chosen one. Although it's considered to be a special honour, you are feeling anxious and fearful of what's coming for you tonight. Only certain parts of the ritual have been revealed to you. After being prepared, you are led out through a large crowd to an alter. The high priest officially presents you to the crowd and receives solemn approval. In the moonlight, you spot the shackles on the alter and the sacred devices that will be used during the ritual. You are then stripped and positioned on the alter to begin the ceremony. Your screams of orgasmic ecstasy are required to announce your virgin offering and summon the god. The skill of the high priest will determine if your offering will be taken tonight.

- Pretend you are surrounded by a crowd of worshippers chanting and watching expectantly
- Adapt as a Black Mass or Aztec Virgin Sacrifice to the Gods and dress accordingly
- Virginity can be offered to a mythical beast, demon, angel or alien
- You can prepare a room with candles and incense or pretend you are out in the middle of a forest clearning
- Cover a table with a blanket as a pretend altar
- Adapt to have a priestess perform the ritual

77 Snake Charmed

You are the sneaky archangel who suggested Adam needed a companion and even helped with her design. The clueless bugger didn't even know what to do with her but you do. Patiently you wait for the right moment. While he went off to play with the animals, the gorgeous Eve was left alone to play with herself. Now is your chance. To avoid scaring her by appearing in your full form, you decided to let your "snake" do the talking first. It knows just how to introduce her to the pleasure features you secretly added to her design. She was slowly starting to discover a few of them herself but you know exactly how to access and operate all the cleverly concealed climax control centres. She came with no operating instructions but, with you at the controls, she'll experience a wealth of knowledge and rapture will take on a whole new meaning. Your snake just needs to charm her, get her to trust you and then let him taste the forbidden fruit in her bush.

- Play a nature CD to help imagine you're in paradise
- Cover yourself in a way that only your "snake" is visible
- Talk to Eve as if you are the snake and encourage her to play with you
- Compliment her luscious curves and let her know you need to get up close and personal to fully appreciate every part of her body
- Eve should play innocent yet mischievously curious
- How will you talk her into putting your snake inside her secret spot?

78 Habit Forming

The convent was isolated and secluded in a remote mountain forest. Absolutely no men were allowed near the cloistered nuns except for the priest who visited once a week to deliver a sermon and hear their confessions. His intense religious convictions gained him respect however the strict and severe penance he administered was deemed by many to be excessively harsh punishment for minor sins. All the nuns feared him but one also found his moral earnestness extremely exciting. She was especially drawn to him after finding an ancient manuscript of sexual sins in an archival vault. The explicit images and detailed depictions of debauchery fueled her erotic fantasies day and night. She even began to touch herself inappropriately. Knowing the extreme nature and sensitivity of her sins, she requested a confession in his private sanctuary. When she arrived, he noticed that her habit seemed to form around her body in a way that accentuated her feminine beauty rather than conceal it. This created a troubling sensation that only worsened when she started to confess her fantasies involving him.

- Set your scene in Medieval, Victorian or modern times
- Start off following the standard confessional procedure
- Make up a juicy fantasy on the fly or write one that you can read as your confession
- Will he need her to demonstrate her self pleasuring activities or just describe them in explicit detail?
- Will her punishment involve a spanking or paddling?
- What activities will she need to perform to receive absolution for her sins?

Stranger Attraction

Sex with a stranger is a common fantasy for both men and women. Although risky, the lure of hot and fast, no strings attached, anonymous sex can be very appealing and arousing to think of. It can be extremely fun to pretend that you've never met before yet find yourselves drawn to each other with a strange attraction. You can find each other in parks, museums, bars, restaurants, stores, parties or even on a bus, subway or train. Flirting, teasing and seducing each other publicly can be very exciting and emotionally stimulating too. You can pretend to be single and meeting a hot hookup or experience the taboo thrill of infidelity without actually straying. Even though a wild and passionate one night stand can be an ecstatic experience, they're usually not as satisfying as you would expect. With a stranger, you may feel more wild and free to fully express your sexuality but not knowing how to stimulate each other in just the right way can lead to disappointment. However, when you roleplay and pretend to be strangers while knowing exactly how to bring each other to orgasm, you get the best of both worlds.

Set the Scene
- Location: different room, hotel, vehicle, bedroom
- Try meeting publicly before secreting away for sex
- Modify your behavior to seem like someone else
- Dress in a new style of clothing and accessories
- Wear a wig, style or even dye your hair
- Use a mask, blindfold or other visual barrier to look/feel anonymous
- Apply a new perfume or cologne

Sexy Suggestions
- Act as if you've never touched or seen each other naked before
- Start out in public with a private location close by to have sex
- Use different names and see if you can remember to call out the right one during the throes of passion
- Try different sex moves but finish with "go to" techniques if required

Personal Notes & Ideas

79 Seduced by Shoes

She was on a cruise vacation and the ship had just docked at an exotic port for a few hours so the tourists could do some shopping. Most of the women went off looking at jewelry stores but she had a thing for shoes and this town was renowned for it's amazing foot fashions. She was looking for some sexy heels or boots and dressed especially for the shopping experience - the shoes needed to go with the outfit she had purchased in the previous layover. The sign for a little shoe shop tucked away in a small side alley seemed to call out to her. She left the main group, entered the shop and was greeted by a striking man who introduced himself as the owner and designer. He stood back and gazed at her beauty before leading her to a luxurious fitting chair. He then knelt before her and said "Before we begin, please allow me to get a feel for your feet so I can get you the perfect fit." He smiled as he noticed her sheer panties beneath her short skirt. With delicate fingers he removed her current shoes and caressed each foot as he gazed into her eyes. He then disappeared into the back room and returned with the most stunning high heeled shoes she'd ever seen. He lovingly placed them on her feet and she almost swooned in pleasure. She didn't want to take them off and wanted to pay for them right away. At the front counter she handed him her credit card but he frowned slightly saying "Sorry Miss, I don't take credit cards." Seeing her heart almost shatter, he casually walked to the door and locked it saying "Perhaps we can come to an arrangement for both of us to be happy."

- Wear stocking and garters, short skirt and sexy panties
- Professionally admire and caress her feet and legs
- Have sex with your clothes and shoes on

80 Torrid Tunnel Ride

It was late when she finally got off work and grabbed the last train for home. She noticed him sitting at the back of the car right when she entered the doors. Luckily there was a seat free facing him. As she was taking her seat, his eyes caught hers causing her legs to weaken. There was an instant attraction that made her heart race with desire. She could feel herself getting more and more aroused as they flirted silently with all the other passengers around them. At each stop, she feared he would leave. As the train emptied, she moved closer to him knowing that he was getting just as excited as she was. There was only two stops left before she had to get off and she was praying the old guy sitting next to him would leave. She couldn't believe it when everyone else exited the train leaving the two of them alone. As soon as the doors closed, they rushed toward each other, embraced and kissed each other passionately. There was an unspoken understanding that it was now or never. Almost out of breath, she panted "I need to get off on the other side of the mountain tunnel so we only have a few minutes" as she reached to undo his zipper. Just as the train entered the tunnel, his thrusting engine entered hers.

- Making out in a real train may be difficult but possible
- Recreate the excitement in your own home by turning out the lights and playing a train sound track
- Make it a quickie - finish before the sound track ends
- Have sex on a sofa or standing up against a wall
- Wear clothing suitable for easy access and keep them on

81 Partner Swap Party

As part of an erotic adventure, they agreed to go on an erotic cruise for couples. There were a variety of live sex shows and games throughout the week. Everyone was encouraged to participate and enjoy getting to know each other intimately. On the final night, there was a special party planned with a cabin card swap game to finish off the evening. For each couple who wanted in, one person was selected to go back to their cabin while the other placed their key card into either a pussy or penis jar. The individuals returning to their cabins were each given a blindfold and instructed to get prepared anyway they wanted then to get on their bed with the blindfold on. It was recommended that they keep it on for as long as possible. Shortly afterwards, the remaining people all select a card from an appropriate jar to determine where they would go and who they would get to play with.

- Flip a coin to determine who is blindfolded
- Pretend to unlock the door and become the unknown lover
- Use different names if desired and alter your voice
- Person with the blindfold takes on a passive or submissive role
- Keep the blindfold on to retain the mystery of who could be pleasuring you

82 Strange Sucker

He passed by the Hole in the Wall strip joint a few times a week. It always seemed to be busy so he figured the entertainment must be pretty good. This thought combined with his erotic curiosity only fueled his desire to stop in some night. While out having a beer with a few guys from the office, one of them started talking about the club and the reason for it's name. Apparently they setup blow job booths in a special room for the strippers to earn extra money while not on stage. Each of the small stalls were large enough to stand in and provide a bit of privacy. And of course, there was a hole positioned at waist height for obvious reasons. Once you slipped enough cash into the payment slot, one of the girls would attend to your need. The guy raved about how exciting it was to have a mysterious woman's mouth and hands pleasuring him without being able to see her. After hearing this, he couldn't resist anymore. He was a sucker for a good cock sucker so he made a quick excuse to leave early and headed over to get some head.

- For extra realism create a barrier between you using cardboard, drywall, plywood or even a sheet
- Make the hole big enough to allow your hands through
- Apply bright red lipstick and nail polish since he will only get to see your hands and lips
- For extra effect, record another woman's voice and create a track list of various oral sex related expressions that you can play on a laptop at different times

83 Sports Bar Score

She was recently divorced and wasn't interested in looking for a new relationship anytime soon. However, she still loved sex and desperately wanted to get laid. Self pleasuring was great and she wouldn't part with her electronic or silicone friends for anything but she craved the touch, feel, smell and taste of a real man. Her friends thought she had turned into a bit of a nymphomaniac now that she was single again but she didn't care because she was finally having some fun again. She especially liked one night stands so she could play the field more. Tonight she decided she was going to score in a local sports bar that seemed to be a gathering place for a lot of attractive guys especially on big game nights. Having tried out a few single guys and being a tad disappointed with their skills, she was determined to trial a married sports fan tonight. Instead of taking on a professional player or a free agent, it would be more fun and challenging to get a married man to play her games. There were a number of positions she had openings for that she was eager to fill.

- Each wear a different style of clothing
- Arrange to meet at a local sports or hotel bar but pretend you don't know each other
- Flirt while watching a sporting event together
- As a married man he should act reluctant at first but eventually falls for her seduction
- For more adventurous sex, make out in the car or hotel room

84 Escort for the Auction

She was a beautiful and well refined escort commanding very high prices for her time. Only the wealthy elite were able to enjoy her exceptional services. Tonight she was at a secret, by invitation only, charity auction that attracted special buyers from around the world. They were all wearing masks and identified only by number. But rather than being with a client, she was one of the main attractions up for bid. Her unrestricted and exclusive services for one year were on offer with a reserve bid starting at $100,000. Considering her normal fee and her amazing erotic skills, this was a bargain. The highest bidder would be able to utilize her services for anything they desired whether it be a girlfriend experience, trophy companion, submissive sexual servant or dominatrix - all subject to the details of the employment contract of course. Even with her many talents and experience, she felt a little nervous as she was blindfolded and led onto the auction block dressed in her finest lingerie. Since her contract was the final item up for sale, the stage was transformed into a large master bedroom ready for immediate use. All the participants had paid an extra viewing fee to see her skills in action and witness her first erotic session with her new employer (master, mistress or both).

- The blindfold helps you imagine the scene and build anticipation
- The auctioneer highlights her assets and sexual skills before starting the bidding
- He can slowly strip her or have her perform various activities to entice higher bids
- Pretend there is a large monitor displaying her intimate details to the audience
- Pretend you are a stranger having sex with her for the first time while she keeps the blindfold on
- You can switch roles with a gigolo on auction

85 Sexy Sisters Share a Screw

Her twin sister just arrived on an international flight for a surprise visit. They cracked open a bottle of wine and sat out on the deck to talk. There was a lot to catch up with since they both left home for universities in different countries. As they laughed and giggled together, the subject of sex inevitably came up. They had both experimented with girls and each other before but her sister preferred women lately while she enjoyed her man. They compared notes on the pleasuring techniques they loved and then shared some of the wild things they had each done with their partners. Their competitive nature came out even while talking about their sex lives. They even tried to out do each other describing their kinkiest fantasies. That's when the idea for their sexy game formed. They would both go out to dinner and then call over her boyfriend for some fun. He knew she had a twin but was going to be in for a double treat tonight. Her sister hid in the bedroom closet while she invited him in and told him about a sex game she had in mind. He eagerly agreed, stripped down then let her blindfold and tie him up on the bed. Barely able to keep herself from laughing, she told him about her lesbian twin sister and the competition they designed involving him. They were both going to make out with him one at a time just until he was ready to come. As the judge of their sexual skills, he just had to lie there and enjoy the pleasure. The winner would get to finish him off any way she liked.

- Avoid talking to him close up and whisper at times as if you're talking to each other
- Get him excited by pretending to pleasure each other while he can only listen to your descriptions of what's happening and imagine the two of you together
- When you're done performing as girl #1, get off the bed and quick change into a different type of lingerie, put your hair up or down, apply lipstick or remove it, apply a new perfume, etc.
- Use different foreplay techniques and movements while pretending to be your twin
- Feel free to experiment with wildly new ideas you've been eager to try

86 Ultimate Poker Night

He was feeling lucky tonight as he arrived at his friend's house to play poker with the gang. The host's wife answered the door and let him in. She was smart, hot and sexy but her husband treated her like crap. During the game she was ordered to serve the guys and she obediently complied. She seemed to submissively wait on her husband's commands and obeyed immediately. As the game heated up, the host was losing and in desperation, offered up his wife's top into the pot as if they were playing strip poker. Although it was intended to be a distraction, everyone eagerly agreed and she ended up losing it. Next came her bottom, then her bra but eventually the stakes got bigger. Instead of clothing, other progressively more intense sensual services were offered into the pot. Finally the other guys were out and he was playing head to head against the host who was sure he had the best hand but not enough chips to force an all in. Anything goes sex with the wife for all the chips was an offer he couldn't resist. It turned out he was going to get lucky in more ways than one. It was going to be her lucky night too.

- Play poker against a computer player who represents her husband
- Have a stack of real poker chips to play with while receiving your rewards
- For each hand specify what kind of sensual treat she will perform or let you do to her if you win
- Continue playing while she attempts to distract you for her husband
- Progressively increase to more intense sex play until the final hand

Wild Westerns

Maybe you played Cowboys and Indians as a kid or you're fascinated by wild western movies with sexy movie stars. Maybe there's something about the wilderness setting, the rugged characters, the clothing, the hot blooded conflict or the frontier attitudes that turns you on. Either way, cowboy, cowgirl and native Indian costumes can be used in a broad range of erotic dress up and roleplay games for couples. While watching a western movie with your partner, take some time to discuss any fantasies you might like to act out.

Set the Scene
- Bales of straw (hay is very prickly) for a pretend hayloft
- In a barn – a clean horse stall or an actual hayloft
- A saddle and a bench to place it on at the right height (think rear entry)
- Outside in a meadow, in some tall grass or under/against a large tree
- In a rustic log cabin with a wood stove or fireplace
- Camping out in sleeping bags next to an open fire under the stars
- Cowboy hat, toy six shooters and of course cowboy boots
- Ankle length skirt, petticoat, lacy corset, pretty bonnet

Sexy Suggestions
- Rope, leather ties and a whip for tie-up games
- Have sex with your cowboy boots and hat on

Personal Notes & Ideas

87 Male Delivery

As a member of the cowboy courier service, he had given an oath to deliver the mail through rain, shine, sleet or snow. It was a dangerous, lonely job riding through the untamed country but it definitely came with its rewards. Many of the homesteads he was dispatched to were tended by single, lonely women. Most of the men were off seeking their fortune for months at a time and he was the one who brought news of their wellbeing. Whether it was good news or bad, he was there to help comfort these lonely women in their time of need. They almost always invited him to come inside where it was warm and cozy. He was looking forward to his next destination, hoping that the young house wife residing there was alone and eagerly expecting the package he had for her. Although the journey to each home was perilous, the risk of being caught by returning husbands added even more excitement to each touch and go encounter. But he got his biggest thrill and sense of job satisfaction from the joy and happiness the women experienced when he came.

- She can wear a pioneer style dress with apron and bonnet or a petticoat
- Adapt as desired to meet in the house, garden, barn or out on the ranch

88 Indian Taker

You had been tracking a ruthless gang of gunmen through the mountain trails for weeks. Earlier in the day you discovered fresh evidence of their cold blooded brutality. A small traveling band of Indians were attacked and robbed. They also kidnapped a young woman. With only a few hours lead time, you quickly set out after the bandits to ensure they didn't escape from your grasp this time. It was nightfall when you eventually tracked them down to their campsite. You could see the Indian woman tied up while the gang drank and argued over who would get to take her first. There were six of them versus just you so the option of dead or alive was going to be an easy choice to make. You carefully planned your shots to target the ones closest to their guns then quickly fired six perfectly aimed rounds. When the smoke cleared from your surprise attack, the woman was the only other person left alive. Now you just have to figure out what you're going to do with her.

- Play as a bounty hunter, sheriff or betrayed gang leader
- Will her pleasures be given as reward or taken as booty

89 Gold Digger

When they struck gold in the mountains, she headed west with many other people looking to strike it rich and make their fortune. However, she wasn't the kind to literally dig for gold. Instead she was determined to use her beauty and cunning to make her dreams come true. Although she owned the establishment, she worked as a regular saloon girl serving drinks so she could keep a look out for men worthy of her attention. It was her preferred way of prospecting for gold. She even had a secret arrangement with the appraiser to inform her about men who came in with a good find. Having learned well from her previous madame, she also united all the other working women in the town to ensure their services were properly valued and that she received a finder's fee for sending them clients she didn't take on personally. For the lucky few, she appeared to have a heart of gold and would do anything they desired as long as they added to her golden nest egg.

- Dress in a old west burlesque costume
- He can play a lucky miner willing to pay anything to enjoy her pleasures or a gun slinger stealing from miners to spend time with her

90 Taken on a Stagecoach

Raised in the city with all its modern conveniences, she was a prim and proper lady from a well to do family. Everyone thought she was out of her mind when she decided to follow a man westward to the far side of the country. Granted he was a successful business man who wanted to marry her but there were other eligible bachelors in the safety of the city. However she was eager to go and escape the predicable life of the city - she desperately wanted adventure and excitement even if it meant roughing it in the wild frontier. She took a steam train for most of the journey before having to transfer onto a stagecoach for a week long ride to her final destination. Even in her most casual riding clothes, she felt extremely overdressed as she surveyed the town while waiting for the stagecoach to pick her up. When it finally arrived she was shocked by how rustic, worn and dirty it looked but she also felt a secret thrill when she noticed the guard riding shotgun. Her fantasy adventure was about to begin and it was taking her straight through rough and remote territory filled with lawless gunmen and hostile natives.

- Pretend your stagecoach has just been hijacked
- Your money and jewelry is not the only thing they want
- Plead to be ransomed to save your life and honour
- Will she be rescued by a handsome sheriff or be ravished by a rugged outlaw

91 Randy on the Range

Randy was a feisty cowgirl who loved being out on the range. She grew up learning how to ride and shoot as well as any other farm hand. With her rope skills she could lasso and hog tie a calf in record time. She could handle herself and any man who dared cross her path not that many men would. Although extremely attractive and itching to sow her wild oats, fear of her father made many men think long and hard about touching her. However, the wilderness, fresh air and sense of freedom on the trail always had an affect on her. Maybe it was the result of riding her horse all day but she couldn't stop thinking of what she wanted to do with the rugged cowboys who worked with her. Usually by nightfall, she was so horny she just had to have one of them. Whether it's out in a meadow, under a tree, on a cot in the cabin or by the camp fire, she is going to have her way with one or more of them. She just needs to separate one from the herd.

- She can dress in any sexy cowgirl or farmer's daughter style outfit
- If the cowboys can't come to play, will she come across an Indian brave enough

92 Rodeo Riding

He was the trainer and talent scout for the rodeo. His specialty was bull riding and he was the best around. It wasn't a total surprise when she showed up at his facilities to apply for a bull riding position. There were many women who could hold their own on a bucking animal but she was the most attractive cowgirl to come in wanting to ride his bulls. However, she would still have to demonstrate her skills on a mechanical bull first before he would let her near his wild beast. Unfortunately her first ride lasted only a few seconds before she got off premature. She pleaded with him to give her another chance because she desperately wanted to be a rodeo star. After considering her sex appeal and his own skills, he agreed to take her on personally to give her some special one on one training in the art of riding. But she would have to do everything he asked of her starting now.

- Get a feel for her leg grip by having her ride you in cowgirl and reverse cowgirl positions
- She should wear her cowgirl outfit with boots and hat while riding him
- Practice attempting to throw her off while she holds on tight until you can't buck anymore

Tantalizing Times

The 1001 Arabian Nights stories have fueled many exotic fantasies involving treasure, power, temptation and seduction all wrapped in a veil of erotic mystery and intrigue. It's easy to imagine palace life as a rich and powerful Sultan, a rebellious princess, an obedient harem girl or even a submissive royal slave. The science fiction and fantasy realms also provide rich playgrounds for adventure and adult play. There are many periods and places throughout time and space with all kinds of erotic elements for our imagination to use. They each offer unique customs, fanciful garments, sultry music and intoxicating sensations of smell, taste and sight that you can use to spice up your fantasies. Mix in some magic (genies, dragons, enchanted artifacts, etc.) or fantastic technological advances and you have all the ingredients for a wild adventure in a far off land or time. There are many types of roleplay ideas you can explore in these enchanted dream worlds. Form an oasis of pleasure in your bedroom tonight and make all your fantasies come true. Forget historical accuracy or scientific limitations as you create your own magical times.

Set the Scene
- Wear silk or satin lingerie – long and flowing robes or gowns
- Use a variety of colorful silk scarves
- Drape sheets or material from the ceiling to form a tent
- Play exotic music – soft and flowing or pulsating with excitement
- Burn incense and light candles or lamps
- Serve bowls of sensual food – fruit, chocolate, honey, oysters
- Enjoy wine or some other refreshing drink
- Persian rugs can make a more authentic scene or become a magic carpet
- Use exotically scented or flavored massage oil
- Adorn yourself with costume jewelry – nipple and body jewelry if you desire
- Have lots and lots of throw pillows

Sexy Suggestions
- Practice various Kama Sutra and Tantric Sex techniques
- Watch Arabian themed movies with lavish costumes and sets
- Explore erotic and historic art depicting harem or palace life
- Read erotic novels involving harem or slave girls
- Take a belly dance or strip tease course

Personal Notes & Ideas

93 Princely Price Paid

She was blindfolded and led up onto the auction block. A hush came over the crowd when she was presented as the next item up for sale. While the other slaves were used by the guards, her virginity was protected above all else. It was highly prized and would translate into a hefty profit when she was sold by her owner. Something much worse than death would befall anyone who touched her. He didn't want to sell her but he needed some quick gold to cover a gambling debt. Before the bidding could commence, the wealthiest customers were given a chance to more closely inspect her. She was stripped completely naked except for her blindfold so they could intimately examine every detail of her soft glistening body. She had been well prepared ahead of time with perfume and luxuriant oils to entice the buyers. After a few minutes of enduring the touch of unknown hands as they squeezed and stroked every part of her, the auction began. A flurry of bids were shouted out but everything stopped when one bid tripled her value to an enormous sum. Her mind raced as she was shrouded in a silken robe and led away.

- The sex slave auction can be set in a variety times and places throughout history or even in a future dark age
- In ancient Rome, you could be bought as a pleasure servant to a powerful senator, a gift to the emperor or as the stakes for the gladiator games
- In ancient Arabia you may become another wive to a wealthy merchant, added to the Sultan's harem or brought to a distant land to be resold at an even higher price
- Other scenarios can be set in ancient Egypt, India, the olden day southern US or even on another planet
- Instead of being purchased outright, your virginity could be auctioned to noblemen at a Victorian brothel

94 Diplomatic Duty

As a royal emissary, he was carefully trained in all the customs he needed to follow when dealing with other foreign leaders. Each and every sovereign specified exacting rules of behaviour to be followed in their presence. Even ambassadors would be sentenced to death if they failed to honour their supreme host properly. After travelling for months by land and sea, he was currently waiting to be received by the Empress of an exotic oriental island. He was on a trade mission of utmost importance to his King. Failure to negotiate an agreement would result in terrible consequences he didn't even want to imagine. This particular assignment was going to be especially challenging considering the strict puritanical moral convictions he was raised to believe. The Empress was fond of toying with diplomats for her personal pleasure. However she would only engage in official intercourse with those who pleased her to the point of orgasm. After being cleaned and prepared by her servants, he was finally led to her throne where he was expected to bow, kiss her feet and then wait for her instructions.

- She should dress in colorful, silky material
- She can request and take any liberty she desires
- Lay on a bench to present yourself for her pleasure
- She should always be on top until she accepts the treaty
- Adapt to any culture past, present or future including alien planets if desired

95 Desert Treats

It's been a long day travelling through the desert but you have finally reached the oasis. Your servants finished setting up your tent before you arrived. After a refreshing bath to clean off the sand, you recline on a mound of lush pillows to relax and prepare for a night of fun. Even in these harsh lands you're not about to give up the pleasures of palace life. A caravan of slaves and guards accompany you on your journey. Various forms of erotic entertainment and a feast of your favourite foods are always made available to fulfill every desire. You clap three times to signal your treasured harem girl to enter – your every wish is her command. The veiled temptress dances seductively as she reveals all her charms. She pampers you with pleasure – succulent fruit, a sensual massage and what ever else you fancy.

- Give the Dance of Seven Veils your own twist
- Watch a belly dance or other erotic dance scene together while serving each other various treats
- Sample delicacies from each other's bodies
- Use the pillows to get into some creative sex positions

96 Her Very Own Man

Ever since she was a little girl she dreamed of having one. They were advertised all the time. Although a fantasy of every girl to have her own, only wealthy women could afford the luxury of owning a man. With modern fertility and robotic technology, they weren't really needed any more. The few that were born were mostly relegated to labouring but some were specially selected for entertainment services or breeding. While some women still opted for "natural" fertilization, most of the choice males were rented by the hour to women seeking unique pleasure sensations that could not yet be replicated artificially or obtained with another woman. Sharing, rentals and other service options were the usual means for indulging - why buy one when you only needed to ride it a few times a week. Of course, there were special benefits to having your own man. Other than the obvious advantage of being able to spoil yourself anytime you desired, it could be fitted with a special collar and brain implant tuned to your mind and body sensors. After some training, the owner could deliver pain or pleasure with just a thought. Eventually they would become addicted to their owner's happiness especially her orgasms. Although she couldn't afford a brand new one, she had saved enough to buy a pre-owned man at a discount when a rich friend decided to upgrade. She would need to think of a good name for it and teach it some new tricks but that would be part of the fun. With the newly reconfigured collar in hand, she couldn't wait to get home and try it out for size.

- Attach a symbolic collar
- Pretend you need to give him detailed instructions or demonstrations on how to pleasure you
- Show him how to use your toys
- What new tricks will you teach him?

97 Packaged for Pleasure

He couldn't wait to get off work, rush home and open the package he'd been eagerly expecting. After months of working overtime and saving every extra dollar, he was finally able to afford her. He had spent many nights on the product website fine tuning every customization option available to make her perfect. She wasn't any ordinary sex doll - she was the most realistic female replica that modern science could create. She came with a sophisticated AI unit to provide both voice recognition and synthesis which enabled complex communication among other things. Although she wasn't a robot, special sensors could detected external stimuli, anticipate desired actions and perform certain types of movements automatically. The actions were controlled by special software modules that evolved from the initial factory settings by adaptive learning. He would have to train her to adjust to his personal preferences but the default settings received exceptional ratings from satisfied customers. When he arrived home, a large box was sitting in the middle of his living room ready to be opened.

- Pretend you are a sophisticated sex doll
- Dress in sexy lingerie and climb into a large cardboard box or other safe container
- Try to remain still and silent until turned on
- Use a slightly robotic voice when responding
- Assist with some movements but remain in any position you are arranged into
- A full inspection and feature test should be performed first (after reading the care and handling instructions)
- When playing be conscious of physical constraints like breathing and muscle fatigue
- Adapt for her to enjoy a male sex doll if desired

Without going to extremes, a little light S/M can be a thrilling addition to your intimate play. The mixed sensations and emotions associated with certain types of painful stimulation can actually be very pleasurable.

Light S/M stimulation includes: biting, scratching, spanking, pinching and hair pulling. Hot candle wax, flogging and other more intense activities require more skill and knowledge to perform safely and well. What types of light S/M activities would you like to experience and in what types of situations? What types of pain play are you fascinated with but are not willing to engage in?

Fairy Tale Fantasies

Set in strange and wondrous locations with fanciful creatures, fairy tales and myths weave stories where mystery, magic and adventure come together to ignite our imagination. In these stories, heroes of all sorts overcome obstacles and risk danger to protect or rescue the innocent. When they succeed, they're usually rewarded with loving gratitude. However, there are also deliciously wicked foes bent on corrupting or perverting the pure of heart for their own deviant pleasures. The good versus evil theme provides a rich playground for adult make believe. With a few tweaks, classic fairy tales or modern variations can be adapted to very erotic roleplaying scenarios where you can explore romantic love or taboo desires in any combination. As you'll discover, not all fairy tales are for kids.

Set the Scene
- Location: bedroom or secluded spot outdoors
- Agree if good or evil will triumph in your scenario
- Read the original story to get familiar with it again
- Dress in costumes to fit the character if desired
- Some scenarios are suited for using BDSM toys

Sexy Suggestions
- Select a special sex toy to be a magical object in the scenario
- Find a collection of erotic fairy tale stories to read to each other
- Work in taboo sex activities like spanking or anal sex if desired

Personal Notes & Ideas

98 Goldilocks Gangbang

Goldilocks was of age so her parents arranged her marriage to a toy maker in the neighbouring village. Although she would be well cared for, she wanted to have more fun before settling down with just one man. She tied her long curly golden hair in blue ribbons and put on a fancy pale blue, lace edged dress that she received years before. She had grown since so her dress looked very short. It showed off her amazing legs above her white knee high socks. She was sure people would be able to see her white knickers but she didn't care. Her breasts had also grown bigger, almost spilling out her top. With her black buckle shoes she looked so sweet and innocent but she was feeling wild and frisky. Rather than riding a carriage to the next village, she decided to take a short cut through the woods. Skipping along the path she came across a building with a sign that read "Adult Toy Shop" and a note on the door with her name on it. The note instructed her to go into the bedroom and choose an item from each of three boxes labelled Pussy, Ass and Mouth. Each box had a note on how to find the one toy that was just right. A final note told her to put on a blindfold if she wanted to be ravished by three bare men at the same time. She giggled with excitement as her fantasy was about to come true.

- She can try out each of the toys by masturbating with them while he secretly watches
- Pretend to be three different men with unique styles of having sex
- Use dildos and vibrators to simulate double or triple penetration as desired
- Use a penis sleeve, extender or strap-on to simulate different penis shapes/sizes
- Warm a bottle of lube to squirt on her at various times to simulate multiple ejaculations and keep her wet
- Doggie style is a great position to be dominated and ravished in this game

99 Three Chubby Piggies

There once was a very bad wolf who prowled late at night searching for a tasty treat to satisfy her appetite. She was feeling especially hungry when she spotted three of her favourite prey and she wanted to devour them. They were chubby and delicious looking piggies that she wanted to feel stuffed inside her. She licked her lips and said "Oh Yummy" as she came closer to them. Quivering in fear, they dashed away from her grip and hid. "Come out and play. We'll have so much fun together" she said. A little voice asked "How can you play with all three of us at the same time?" She tracked the voice and sweetly replied "It'll be my pleasure to show you" as she snatched two of them one in each hand. The biggest pig got away but she knew he was watching her. She basted the first and got him all greasy before puckering up and sliding him in slowly. Delightful squeals penetrated the night. She was already salivating as she worked the second one past her wet lips. They felt good but she wasn't filled up completely yet so she went hunting for the last one. She called out "I won't bite, I just want to lick and suck on you a bit." She found him buried in some clothes and zipped right in to catch him in her mouth. He was almost too big to get down her throat. As she huffed and puffed with his size, he worked to wiggle the other piggies free before eating her too.

- She can play dressed as a wolf or cougar (lion, tiger, lynx)
- Use a butt plug and a dildo or vibrator as pig 1 & 2
- He plays as the big pig watching his friends swallowed
- While he watches, she masturbates before catching him

100 Naughty in Neverland

Although Peter Pan remained a boy, Wendy had grown up and was having thoughts and feelings of an adult nature. Playing doctor together was still fun and she especially enjoyed when he pretended to be a puppy dog licking her all over. But, since Peter's peter couldn't grow either, she had to find other ways to satisfy her urges. That's when she started fantasizing about Captain Hook. She secretly spied on him with a telescope and watched him masturbate in his cabin on the ship. He would swap his hook for a strange device that he used to pleasure himself with. There were times she saw him with a different attachment that he used to threaten the crew. For some reason, the thought of him using it on her made her body ache with desire. She imagined herself tied to the mast while he defiled her in front of the entire crew. She pleasured herself to thoughts of being ravished by the cruel captain. Then one day while spying on him, she saw him spying on her so she started slowly stripping and fondling herself hoping to entice him to come and get her.

- Tied and blind folded, she begs him not to use his special tool
- Pretend that the crew watches as he roughly strips and ravishes her
- While walking the plank she offers to become a pirate wench and describes all the things she'd be willing to do for the captain

101 Ogregasm

As an Amazonian warrior, no man was able to match her sexual appetite. They cowered in her presence and shrivelled in her embrace. Upon penetration, their spears softened much too quickly and could not thrust to the depths of her desire. She thought all hope lost but then heard of an ogre living in a distant land. The legend told of a cruel giant with a cyclops sprouting from his thighs. The vile creature terrified women throughout the region. It was rumoured that he was a perverted beast that violated them with depraved acts of lust. All the women were released unharmed except for their reputation. For some mysterious reason, they all wandered into the woods alone after their encounter. The stories and engravings of this monster intrigued her so she set off on a quest to capture him. She tracked him down and found him sleeping in his cave. With utmost stealth she shackled him to his bed. Just as she finished restraining him, he awoke with a roar shaking the bed struggling to get free. She pounced on him and squeezed her legs around his waist. As she rode his bucking body, she could feel the fabled snake between his legs grow stiff and hard. His eyes focused on her bouncing breasts and he slowly calmed down mesmerized by her beauty. When he finally settled, she looked him in the eyes and said "I hear you like to eat women." He grunted a reply "I don't eat women, I just like to lick and suck on them because they taste good." She smiled and said "Well you're going to like the way I taste" as she slid up to straddle his face. As he started to devour her, she said "And I think your giant snake will feel right at home in my cave too."

- He can wear a loin cloth or cave man costume
- She can be dressed as an Amazonian warrior or in black leather bra and mini-skirt
- She can tease and torment her captive beast before enjoying rough and wild sex

102 School Spirit

It was like ancient history but every cheerleader knew the story and pledged to uphold the tradition. Whether the stories were true or not, they had never missed a championship game and rarely lost the final. In fact they never lost on their home field. However it wasn't always this way. In fact, before that special night, their puritanical school never won ever. Since then, the string of first and second place trophies became a testament to their belief that what they did worked. Players and coaches came and went but the school kept on winning. While most people thought it was due to their strict religious practices, only the cheerleaders knew of the pre-game activity that provided their team with this spectacular sequence of victories. It was an initiation requirement for all cheerleaders to ensure their secrecy. Once it was performed, nobody would admit to what they had done. All they had to do was leave one of the girls in the change room alone before the game started. The team mascot would mysteriously appear, the girl would be overcome with lust and they would ravish each other. When they were done, he would vanish like a ghost leaving her with just a smile on her face. After all the new girls were initiated, they would pick names from a hat. Tonight you've been picked and you can't wait.

- Pretend your bathroom is a school change room
- Dress in a cheerleader outfit or just a towel fresh from a shower
- He can dress as any sexy mascot with the costume adapted for easy access
- Have sex while in costume

103 Arousing Apparition

It was a dark and stormy night with huge streaks of lightning piercing the sky. He was driving just a little too fast down the deserted country road when he came across a woman in white appearing right in front of him. Swerving hard, he skidded into the ditch. Still shaken from the crash, he rushed out into the rain to check on the woman but saw no sign of her. Just then a flash of lightning streaked and lit up an old house across the road - the first he'd seen in hours. And for a brief instant he thought he saw the woman in the doorway. When he went to the house, the door was open but no one answered his calls. The house was pitch black except for a glow of light upstairs. It led him to the master bedroom with a single candle on the night stand. Next to it was an old note that told of a bride who mysteriously died before consummating her marriage. The husband sold his soul to get her back but she returned as a ghost with a single purpose. Although the husband loved her deeply, he could not bring himself to give her what she desired and left the house never to return. She was now condemned to haunt the house until a man proved his love for her. Dressed in a silky white nightie, she now lures men into her bedroom to arouse them with her beauty and seduce them into her carnal embrace. If the man is able to satisfy her craving, she would then have the release she needs to rest in peace. But if she's not sent to heaven, there will be hell to pay. As he finished reading, he had an overwhelming urge to strip down and crawl into the bed. Just as he did, the candle went out and her image appeared.

- Enjoy during an actual storm or play a thunder and rain nature CD
- Experiment with glow sticks, a strobe or black light for a spooky effect
- Watch a good horror movie or read each other a ghost story to set the mood

104 Red Riding Hood Gets Eaten

It was getting late and she still had to get home. Her grandmother warned her about being alone in the woods at night especially during a full moon. She had been told the stories all throughout her childhood about a vile beast that takes innocent young ladies. But she was a woman now and could handle herself in many different ways. Besides, she always carried a little protection. Tonight, under her cape she was dressed to kill in a special red outfit and she was going out to hunt. She strolled down the path with a seductive sway to her hips teasing her prey with her sexy innocence. While she appeared calm, her body was trembling with hot desire for this creature that dominated her dreams and forced entry in her fantasies. She knew he wouldn't be able to resist her allure. With a lustful growl, he pounced on her and knocked her to the ground onto her hands and knees. She felt him trying to mount her as she struggled under him. While he was trying to tear at her under garments, she got her chance and quickly spun around into a missionary position with her gun pointed right at him. He snarled "I want to fuck you so bad." She spread her legs and said "First you're going to eat me like it says in the book."

- Wear red lingerie (crotchless panties) with a hooded cape
- "My what a big tongue you have." "Better to lick you with."
- Enjoy oral sex and then intercourse doggie style
- Take him down using a silver vibrating bullet
- Conquer the wolf man using a silver (chrome) dildo or butt plug
- For more kinky play, turn him into your pet with a collar and leash

105 Medusa's Dildo Collection

He watched in horror as his warrior friend succumbed to her sexual powers. The poor soul knew the legends of Medusa and the risk of attempting to be the first man to claim her virginity. The promise of ever lasting pleasure as her king lured men from all the lands to their doom. The imminent demise of his loyal friend was a sacrifice he had to make to learn her secrets. He needed to know how to penetrate her defences and unlock her treasure box. With intense desire, he observed how she worked her magic on an all too willing victim. With lust in his loins, the soldier was drawn to her seductive body - his manhood raging and ready for battle. She parted her legs inviting his onslaught but as soon as his penis touched her pubic hairs, his entire body started turning into glass. With a laugh, she broke off his penis and pushed his body off her bed to shatter on the marble floor. He continued to watch as she masturbated with her glass trophy. Sated from her orgasm, he heard her say "I wish they would at least try to pleasure me before trying to stick it in." With mystical insight, the arcane scripture finally made sense. There was a dire warning but only three words could be deciphered "Cut Off Head." It was so obvious now. Instead of killing her, he needed to trim her evil pubic hairs and pleasure her with his head between her legs. With one or two orgasms to weaken her powers, she would accept him into her paradise.

- She can dress as a Goddess or ancient queen
- He can dress as a Greek warrior or gladiator
- Masturbate and enjoy foreplay using a glass dildo
- Perform oral sex on each other until she begs for him to be inside her

106 Irresistible Sleeping Beauty

Her parents the King and Queen never told her about the curse of the Wicked Witch. On the day of her birth the witch proclaimed "She is protected from my powers while she remains pure and innocent. However, once her hymen is pricked, she will fall into an everlasting deep sleep and never age a day." A special castle was built for her and all men were banished from it. Female guards patrolled the grounds and she was made to wear a chastity belt if she went outside the castle walls. She was being groomed to be a virgin queen (with female lovers if she desired). However, one day while secretly masturbating in the tower bedroom, she noticed a small chest on the bookshelf. Curious, she opened it to find a stash of erotic literature with pictures and a sensually shaped, smooth glass object. She started reading, discovered what the glass dildo was for and couldn't resist trying it. As soon as she pushed it in, she fell asleep dreaming of the handsome stud in the story. The kingdom was in despair. They laid her to rest in the tower bedroom without knowing the one crucial loophole in the curse - if another prince takes her while sleeping, the two of them will fall magically in love and live happily ever after. Many years later, a handsome and horny young prince finds her irresistible.

- Both dress as royalty with crowns if desired
- She wears lingerie or a silk gown that opens in the front
- He tries to awaken her with his kisses, caresses and licks
- She only awakes when he sheaves his manhood into her

107 Snow White and the Wicked Queen

Through her magic mirror, the Wicked Queen watched with glee as the seven dwarves laid Snow White to rest in a glass coffin. They left her to be in peace out in the middle of the forest. Unfortunately she still looked beautiful and innocent which left the queen feeling unsatisfied and frustrated. There was something about that poison spell that wasn't working as planned. She looked up the spell in her book of evil magic and was horrified to see the warning in small print - Snow White would remain in a timeless state of beauty until she was deflowered by a person of royal blood and then she would awaken to fall madly in love with them. The Queen exploded in a fit of rage but then had a delightfully devious thought - she was of royal blood. With a flick of her magic wand, she transformed her pussy into a magnificent example of manhood just right for the job she had in mind. With another wave of her wand, she was transported into the middle of the forest beside Snow White. Her new prick instantly swelled with lecherous intent. Her deviant desire to defile Snow White aroused her more than she expected. She wanted to take pleasure enjoying her depraved urges before ravishing her conquest.

- She wears a Snow White costume and pretends to be in a deep sleep
- He wears a black evil witch or wicked queen costume
- With pretend magic and a strap-on, you can switch roles

108 Ravishing the Rich

It was a well know secret, among the noble women at least, that Robin Hood was an amazing lover. The masked marauder had an arrow that could make any woman quiver with pleasure. His legendary skills enabled him to hit the target every time. But he didn't come for free - he expected to be paid for his services. However, to ensure the honour of each client was protected in case he was seen entering or leaving their home, he robbed from the rich husbands after ravishing their wives. The ruse made him a wanted man throughout the land. Hearing of his crimes and reputation separately, both the sheriff and his wife wanted him desperately. While her husband was hunting the forest for the fugitive, she sent a special coded invitation for the mysterious lover to plunder her treasure box.

- Dress in a Victorian style gown, exotic lingerie or corset
- He can wear a mask and cape

109 Gold Fingering Genie

Working as a mild mannered jewelry store owner by day, part super villain and super hero by night, he was a gold genie with a special talent turned obsession. Over the many years of his existence as a genie, he fondly remembered the beautiful princess Jasmine who freed him after being her love slave for just three decades. In those few years, he developed a taste for pleasuring her and feeling the thrill of her sexual energy as it passed through his body. He adored watching her even when she entertained various princes, diplomats and soldiers in her bed chamber. But while they could not fully satisfy her, his magic fingers could. Before she released him, she made him promise to use his gift and follow his voyeuristic passion. She wanted him to bring pleasure to women throughout the world especially those left unfulfilled by their lovers. While in his disguise fitting rings and jewelry on his customers, he used his powers to sense their future so he could magically show up if and when they needed him. He would enjoy watching his customers have sex. Then, after the frustrated woman finished trying to satisfy herself while her lover slept, he would appear and use his gold fingers to give her an explosive orgasm. Of course they always assumed he was part of a wild wet dream and in a sense he was.

- Assume you have just watched a woman have sex
- Pretend her lover just rolled over to sleep
- Watch her masturbate then appear to give her a G-spot orgasm using your fingers
- Ever so grateful, she polishes your golden knob

110 Naughty on the North Pole

Although her husband enjoyed his role as a chubby old man delivering toys around the world, she preferred a young and sexy look for herself. It helped keep her young at heart and mind too. While he spent most of the year working hard to bring joy and happiness to the world, she wasn't just sitting around by the fire. However, she had a different idea on how to make people smile contentedly and it didn't come just once a year. She liked toys too but believed both naughty and nice girls deserved the ones she made. Being a little naughty herself, she hand selected a team of elves to create a top secret workshop to design gifts of pure pleasure. Of course they had to be creatively disguised and only sent to the women on her naughty list. The crafty elves made them look like icicles, candy canes, decorative ornaments and even one that looked like the north pole. Unfortunately, although she used her toys whenever she could, she would only risk going to the workshop to personally test new prototype toys on just one special night each year. The head elf would help perform the tests until she was completely satisfied with them.

- Get a few new sex toys as prototypes to test
- Dress up in sexy red lingerie or a Mrs. Claus outfit
- He can dress in green as an elf eager to please

111 First Contact

While driving down a deserted highway late at night, she was suddenly blinded by a bright pulsing light that seemed to float onto the road ahead of her. She stomped on the brakes and skidded to a stop. With her adrenaline pumping, she ventured out of her car to see what she almost hit. A greenish fog obscured her vision even though the light was so intense. Then, like a deer in the headlights, she froze when three alien creatures emerged from the gloom. She just stood there unable to run as they approached, took her by the arms and led her into their ship. They were humanoid type creatures who were able to speak to her although in a slightly awkward voice. She was informed that they had monitored Earth's communications to learn as much as they could but now needed to examine a human in more detail. They also told her they were on an interstellar mission to document other intelligent races that may have been seeded throughout the galaxy by a common ancestor. That was why they appeared very similar to humans but they needed to perform various tests to verify their theory. In an almost hypnotic state, she let them remove her clothes and strap her onto an examination table. Then after attaching a device to her head to monitor brain activity, they laid out a variety of probes and stimulation devices. The lead examiner seemed to smile when a bleep of excitement registered on his equipment.

- Pretend that other aliens are watching the procedure
- Stimulate every erogenous zone in different ways to record the effect on the subject
- The aliens are secretly perfecting an orgasm device to control the human race
- Buy or make an alien costume if desired
- Use a variety of sex toys and other items for creative pleasuring
- Use a french tickler or penis sleeve for an alien look and feel if intercourse is part of the required research

Wanton Witches & Wizards

When you want to bring some magic into your love life, try roleplaying a sexual fantasy with a witch or warlock theme. There are good and bad witches so you can include a range of erotic ideas to suit any taste. There are some amazing and authentic looking witch costumes to help get you into character. Just showing up in the bedroom with a sexy witch costume can be very hot and exciting. Being a naughty little wicked witch can be very erotic. Or pretend to be a wizard practicing your sorcery by tapping the sexual energy of mortals to power your spells. When you get into character you may find yourself doing things your secretly desired but were afraid to try. Dress up as a sexy witch and see what kind of magic you can bring to your bedroom games. As you play with each other, your foreplay can be sweet and sensual or kinky and nasty.

Set the Scene

- Play eerie background music or sound effects
- Selection of magic wands (glass dildo, vibrators, butt plugs, riding crop)
- Bubbly potion or magic elixir (champagne, wine, herbal enhancer)
- Cover your bed in red satin sheets with a black comforter
- Candles and incense indoors or play outside during a full moon
- Erotic "torture" devices (feather, nipple clamps, whip, paddle, hot wax)
- Exotic witches brew ingredients (grapes, oysters, dark chocolate, liquors, gummy worms, candy spiders, etc.)

Sexy Suggestions

- Find some love spells or sexy incantations or make up some of your own erotic poems
- Write them in a special journal style book customized with symbolic artwork or crystals
- Give yourself a mystical name for your character
- Use anointing substances (flavored oils, syrup, stimulating lubes, lipstick, body paint) as part of your foreplay ritual
- Explore bondage equipment and even electro-stimulation wands if desired

Personal Notes & Ideas

112 Lecherous Lessons

She was warned that he was a wise but wicked wizard who would take advantage of her youthful innocence. Her coven promised that she would be taught all the spells she needed to be a good witch. Although she wanted to know all their secrets, she wanted to become an all powerful sorceress and craved knowledge of the dark arts too. The wizard trained her to tap into her own sexual energy but it only stimulated her desire for more. The carnal knowledge he tempted her with was forbidden but she was eager to experience all its erotic secrets whatever the out come. She delved deep into his ancient books each with lewd depictions of ritualistic ceremonies. They described a cosmic connection that occurred when physical stimulation energized the body just right. She practiced on her own while he observed and was able to get good results. However, tonight there would be a full moon and the wizard pledged to empower her dark magic with his own during a special initiation ceremony. She lusted for the power he promised and was willing to sacrifice her innocence, purity and virginity to get it. With all the skills she had been taught, she energized the wizard's wand and opened herself to be filled completely with the strength of his magic essence.

- Look through books of erotic art or sex positions
- Dress as an older wizard with a greying beard
- Build your sexual energy as much as possible with various foreplay techniques
- Use his penis as a magic wand to complete the ritual
- Adjust the story to open a dark portal (anal sex)

113 Simultaneous Supernatural Climax

It was foretold that a new Queen of Darkness would be conceived tonight during the full moon exactly at the stroke of midnight. Covens around the world prepared for years for this sacred night. Success would bring huge rewards but failure came with dire consequences. Failure to conceive exactly at the crucial time would immediately give rise to a demonic beast with an insatiable lust to violate every witch in sight for all eternity. As the chosen one for her coven, she trained to be in tune with the powers of her sexuality. Special exercises and self practice combined with live demonstrations ensured she knew how to get the job done. She learned all the tricks to make a man come on command. She needed to remain a virgin but required all the skills of a courtesan to ensure a simultaneous climax with the seed provider. He had to be a virgin as well and was captured long ago to ensure his purity. When she entered the sacred circle, she saw him for the first time tied to the alter naked. As the coven chanted incantations, she partially disrobed and straddled him. She fed him the special brews and potions prepared for both of them then began to build her arousal by rubbing her body against his. He was hard and throbbing when the time came for her to impale herself with his manhood. The other witches watched and counted down as she worked her body on his. She was ready with her finger to trigger his explosion at exactly the right moment.

- Set a count down timer for 5 minutes when ready
- If she can't make him ejaculate at the right time, he rips free of his bondage and ravishes her using fingers, dildos and vibrators to bring her to multiple orgasms

114 Haunted House Servant

Although she was an evil and wicked witch, her beautiful body still ached with sexual cravings that needed to be satisfied. If she could find the right victim, she could indulge a few of her other deviant desires too. As bad luck would have it, she sensed a perfect pleasuring candidate about to drive by her lonely home. With a flick of her wand, the engine sputtered and died. As the driver emerged from his stricken car she instantly knew he would make a fine servant to service all her needs and desires. The only problem was that he had to freely enter her haunted lair before she could bewitch him and take control of his mind, body and soul. Reading his thoughts, she quickly discovered that his innocence was only physical and his fantasies were of a much darker nature. With a wicked laugh she transformed herself into the sweet young innocent girl of his dreams and lured him into her trap. Now, with him tied up and struggling, she revealed her true self. But before she cast a spell to make him an obedient slave, she decided to have some fun twisting his kinky ideas for her own perverse pleasure. His training could wait until she finished playing with him.

- Wear demure looking clothing over a sexy black leather or lingerie outfit so you can transform from innocent girl to wicked witch
- Pretend you can read and control his mind and make him believe anything you desire

115 Pagan Pleasure Practice

You are a pre-christian era Pagan witch living outside a small rural village and are well know and respected for your natural remedies. To keep the villagers healthy and happy you promote sexual wellbeing and erotic healing practices. Today a woman has requested your help with her husband. You've been asked to help this man improve his potency, virility and lovemaking skills. With hands on, guided instruction, you will train him in the sensual art of pleasuring a woman and expressing his own intimate desires. Introduce him to new sexual techniques and special orgasmic remedies.

- Invite him into a an exotic room lit with aromatic candles
- Guide him to sensually and intimately explore your body and his own
- Give him samples of massage and clitoral stimulation oils to try
- Demonstrate manual and oral stimulation and let him practice on you
- Sample a variety of exotic sounding aphrodisiacs
- Show him how to use a selection of dildos "made" from magical substances (crystal, vegetables, wood, marble, ivory, unicorn horn, etc.)

116 Demon Dildo Devotion

You're a novice witch on a quest to master the dark arts and become a great sorceress. While combing through an old wizard's tomb searching for new spells and potion recipes, you discover a box with an odd shaped object and a scroll. When you pick up the object it starts to glow and vibrate. The scroll, covered with images of fornicating demons and beasts, provides detailed instructions for using the mystical object. Reading the ancient text, you discover that you are now in possession of a demon dildo. Lusting for its power, you're willing to sacrifice your virginity to tap the erotic energy permeating this ancient artifact. Back in your lair, you prepare for the deflowering ritual specified on the scroll. As you start to masturbate with the object and pledge your devotion to the demon, you feel it transform in and around you. The creature (devil, vampire, werewolf, dragon) is insatiable as it penetrates deep into your body to fuse its essence with yours. The beast takes you again and again throughout the night but disappears at the first light of dawn.

- Begin with a dildo or vibrator and have your partner dressed as a demon creature enter the scene (and you) when you call out a special phrase

117 Cat Love

As you are skimming through a new spell book, your feline familiar jumps onto your lap, curls up and begins purring. The warmth and intense vibration it's creating starts to have an incredibly arousing affect. As if by magic, the next spell you come across gives you the ability to transform your demon companion into an ideal sex partner to satisfy all your erotic desires. Stroking your pussy, you communicate your plans for it to become your lover. You pick up your cat and move it to your bed before gathering the necessary potions, charms and instruments you'll need to cast the spell. Before reciting the incantation, you need to bring yourself to a heightened state of excitement and make your body irresistible to the demon. Your sexual energy will power its metamorphosis and allow your demon to come out and play before returning back to is normal form when you are fully satiated.

- Play as a witch or warlock
- Your partner can dress in a cat costume if desired
- Retain a few cat traits initially and enjoy some licking and purring together

118 Carnal Confessions

You have been apprehended for the heinous crimes of practicing witchcraft and cavorting with the devil. Before you can be sentenced and punished for your sins, you need to confess all the lurid details of your satanic sex rituals and admit that you are indeed a wicked witch. A special inquisitor was summoned to extract your confession using any means necessary. The guards come and blindfold you to protect the court officials from your seductive powers of mind control. You are then moved from the dungeon cell to a different chamber where you are shackled and prepared for the inquisition. You sense other people in the room who will be observing and documenting the procedure in explicit detail. First you'll be stripped bare and shamefully exposed then violated in perverse ways to gauge your response. Signs of arousal will incriminate you. An orgasm will seal your fate. Your only way to avoid the disgraceful torment is to describe all the nasty activities you engaged in so that your soul can be saved. To avoid the torture of prolonged stimulation you may even have to recount imaginary events from your deepest, darkest fantasies.

- Will you need to endure *trial* by judge and jury too?
- Can you weave an erotic tale to seduce and bewitch everyone in the room
- Punishment may include being impaled on a huge holy "stake"
- Adapt for witch or warlock

119 Convent Convert

He is the headmaster and devote priest at a small convent. They had just received a new girl into their order. She appeared shy and innocent but he experienced ominous feelings whenever she came around him. That was also the time when he started to be haunted by dreams of extreme lust – lewd and nasty acts of depravity that made him recoil in disgust. He doubled his prayers to banish these sexual demons from his mind but they seemed to only intensify his erotic thoughts. Working late to avoid the nightmares, he noticed candle light coming from within the chapel. Outraged that anyone would be in there without his permission, he rushed over and burst through the doors to catch the intruder. He was shocked to see the new girl naked, bent over the alter and in the middle of a black magic ritual. She was deep in a trance reciting lurid offerings to the devil. As he approached her, he couldn't help noticing a birch switch laid out next to her. She needed to be punished so he picked it up but something wasn't right. Did she plan this on purpose? Was he being used for her dark pleasure or something even more sinister? Before he could think, the urge to whip her took over and sealed his fate as her satanic sex slave.

- Start off slow if using an actual switch
- Complete the conversion ritual with intercourse or anal sex

Voracious Vampires

Dracula and all the creepy vampire variations have haunted and fascinated our imaginations for ages. Their hypnotic power to seduce others with elegant charm and sophistication inspires our own desire for control and submission. Just imagine having the ability to make others submit to your will and satisfy your needs. To have the power to manipulate their thoughts and feelings so they crave your touch, your kiss, your bite … your love. Or be the helpless victim as your vampire lover takes possession of your mind and body. It knows your inner most secret desires and breaks down all your inhibitions … you're powerless to resist its deviant and lascivious intentions. Add a bit of bite to your bedroom games and try roleplaying as a sexy vampire and willing victim tonight. Experience the erotic thrill of being predator or prey.

Set the Scene
- Location: bedroom, dark alley or by an old graveyard
- Nighttime is the best for the classic vampire
- Set the mood with candlelight and erie music
- Vampire costume with a set of fangs
- White dress or nightgown for the vampire bride
- Red wine or liquor for fake blood
- Bible, 'holy' lube, silicone or glass 'stake' for the vampire hunter
- Bondage cuffs or restraints

Sexy Suggestions
- Adapt a scene from one of your favorite movies or books
- You can make the storyline eerie and scary or turn it into a sexy spoof
- Creatively weave sex into the plot by pretending orgasmic energy is the life force that the vampire hungers for
- Vampire and prey scenarios are great for playing with dominance and submission

Personal Notes & Ideas

120 This Job Will Suck

When he first entered the seminary to become a priest, he could never imagine the holy work he would be called upon to perform. Due to the secret nature of this particular affliction, he had never heard about the practice of erotic exorcism. Only a few hand selected members of the clergy were made aware of the semen sucker scourge and even fewer taught how to intervene. Situations requiring this type of intervention were rare but were growing more frequent lately. It was a tough job but they had trained him well and he had the skills and equipment required to get it done. He talked with the husband briefly before entering the bedroom and locking the door. The man's wife was tied to the bed as instructed. She looked at him calmly, smiled sweetly and pleaded "Please untie me. I'll be a good girl and do anything you want." Her innocent act didn't fool him - he knew she was turning into one of them. She would use any and every type of seductive ploy to entice him to give up his sexual essence before the ritual was complete. He needed to make her orgasm while penetrating her with his man stake. But, if she made him orgasm first, her transformation would be complete. Then, with her lustful powers fully energized, they would all be doomed. While she was begging for him to let her suck his cock, he prepared his holy lube, glass dildo and other exotic stimulators. While resisting all her attempts to excite him, he would drive her into a frenzy of animal lust before venturing in to finish the job.

- Sensually apply 'holy' lube to her body
- Try a clitoral excitement oil if desired
- Pretend various types of foreplay activities are part of an erotic cleansing ritual
- She should talk dirty and try to get him to cum first
- Start sweet and seductive at first then get more explicit and dirty

121 Suck Master

Your nocturnal master appears before you. You drop to your knees to await his commands. Tonight he has promised to transform you into his immortal bride. He will nourish himself on your female essence before allowing you to suck on him. Taunting you with his mighty sceptre, you must prove your worthiness before he allows you to swallow his demon elixir. During your last night as a human, he will revel in your sexual torment as he repeatedly teases you to the brink of orgasmic ecstasy. Once your juices are flowing hot and your erotic energy has peaked, he will allow you to climax as he devours your explosive release. He will savour the power of your orgasms until you are totally drained and he has quenched his thirst. Only then will he allow you the pleasure of receiving his special gift.

- Dress in a sexy "virginal" white nightgown or lingerie
- He makes her perform wicked acts to defile her innocence
- He uses sex toys and his fingers to tease her then licks her to multiple orgasms
- He "deflowers" her but withdraws for her to suck him if she's been good

122 Her Stakes Now

You've been hunting the Queen of Darkness in her lair but night has fallen and you stumbled into her trap. Now under her control, you are bound and displayed for her sadistic pleasure. You see her looking through your bag of vampire slaying implements and notice that she has quite an exotic collection of special devices herself. Hot flashes of her wicked intentions flicker through your mind – fear mixes with excitement as you watch her approach. You're now her play thing and she's going to use your own tools on you for her pleasure. But when she's finished playing, will she suck and drain you until you collapse or make you service her until she's satiated? Or can you still escape and impale her on your man stake before she pegs you with hers?

- Explore various types of BDSM play or extended teasing foreplay
- Use a variety of glass or silicone dildos as stakes
- Butt plugs or prostate massager if desired
- Double ended dildo or strap-on for role reversal play

123 Wet Dream Feast

Sleeping comfortably you suddenly become aware you're having the most erotic dream. You can't open your eyes but you sense you're not alone. Images of hot sex and screams of ecstasy distract you as you struggle to regain full consciousness. It feels like someone is stroking and licking you. You're about to orgasm – do you lay back and enjoy the sensation or fight harder to wake up? The warm lapping and sucking between your legs feels incredible but somehow wrong at the same time. You instinctively know that if you open your eyes the exquisite pleasure will stop immediately and you'll be confronted with something wicked.

- The prey (male or female) lays naked in bed with eyes closed
- The vampire can whisper a sexy description of a hot sex scene or fantasy
- Turn on a porn video with no sound then slowly increase the volume
- Stroke and lick various erogenous zones before oral sex
- If the victim opens their eyes stop and switch to other activities like intercourse

Stimulating Hot Scenarios

In this section, you'll discover inspiring and creative ideas for coming up with your own erotic roleplay scenarios. There are so many possibilities for enhancing your passion play that it can be hard to choose. Sometimes it's easier and more fun to come up with a new idea together when you're given a constraint to work within. Each of the following ideas provide a subject, category or topic to guide the selection of your own roleplay characters, settings and activities. Both of you should attempt to come up with your own ideas separately and then decide which one to do first. Once you pick one, look up some more background information if necessary and work out an appropriate scenario. Keep in mind that nothing has to be kept factual or accurate in your roleplay unless you really want it to be and, even then, you'll still want to keep it light hearted and fun for both of you. Let your imagination run wild as you think of ways to adapt it into an erotic and sexual scenario. To add an extra twist, consider switching the normal male and female roles.

When adapting your scenario for an erotic escapade in or out of the bedroom, think about the types of foreplay and sex play you want to enjoy as well as the range of emotions you want to experience. Try to come up with a way to include various sex toys and pleasuring accessories if desired. You can also integrate various fetish type items or props that you find sexy or erotic. Keep things simple at first and add more details if you find the scenario works for both of you. Having more delicious frisky fun together is the ultimate goal.

Passionate Politicians

Power is an aphrodisiac for many people - both possessing it and being possessed by it. Mix in the high profile public nature of certain political positions and you have a very attractive combination. Politicians can be great leaders with strong convictions or corrupt officials that use their power for personal gain and pleasure. Political command and control can even be used for more sinister purposes which can also be strangely seductive in itself. Various levels and types of politicians (mayor, governor, senator, minister, president, dictator, etc.) can play a role in your erotic fantasy. Choose a political leader from the past, present or future who intrigues or inspires you in some way. They can be from any country or civilization.

- Look up some information about their personality
- Watch a biography or documentary about the person
- Complementary player can be their assistant, spouse, rival or even another foreign leader

Comic Book Character

Many of the classic super heroes and villains started off as comic book characters. Many cartoons, television series and movies have been made based on these characters. Most of them have some sort of love story weaved through the various plots and a few even have explicit sexual adaptations available. Choose a comic book or comic strip character to play the central role in your erotic scenario. You can even transform "wholesome" family style comics into sexy scenarios. You loved reading them as a kid now you enjoy them even more as an adult.

- Rent, buy or make a suitable costume
- Read the comic or watch a show together
- See if you can find any erotic adaptations
- The complimentary character can be the normal love interest, a rival, a modified side kick or an unusual alternate target of affection

Randy Royalty

Royalty throughout the ages has provided a rich and fertile list of personalities that you can use in your erotic roleplay scenarios. Even the abstract idea of being in absolute control is seductive. You have the wealth and power to get anything you desire. Elegance, luxury and pleasure abound. Whether a regal king, queen, prince, princess or emperor, you are the center of attention. Some were cruel and ruthless while others captured the hearts and minds of their subjects with their beauty or leadership qualities. Choose a specific person of royalty to be the main character in your erotic scenario. They can be anyone from the past or present in any country or civilization.

- Find out any information you can about the details of their life and how they behaved
- Choose a scandal if any to base your scenario on
- Complimentary character can be a servant, aristocrat, artisan or royalty from another country

Arousing Artists

Master painters and sculptors throughout history have created dazzling artistic achievements that can capture our hearts and minds. With skilled hands and an eye for beauty, they can inspire our own passion, fascination and curiosity. Great art can stimulate our imagination and encourage our own creativity. Consider being the subject for one of their more romantic or erotic master pieces. Choose a famous artist to base a roleplay scenario on. Select one based on their life's work or just a single piece of their art that you personally love. Pretend to be the artist and subject during an intensely sensual session or design a scenario based on what is represented by a specific piece of art.

- Even if you are not artistically inclined, focusing on your partner in an erotic pose while you attempt to draw or paint them can be very rewarding for both of you
- As a date together, visit a museum or gallery displaying the works of various artists before making your choice
- Look up the artist and some of their work online to get more details about their history and background
- Do an internet search for "erotic art" to find an inspiring image, scene or pose

Exotic Customs & Cultures

With all the books, magazines, movies and television shows portraying and documenting all the diverse exotic cultures and customs around the world, you're bound to come across a few that captivate your erotic imagination. The novel foods, styles of dress, entertainment, religious customs, laws, marriage practices, festivals and celebrations can each provide you with a rich assortment of ingredients to spice up your love play. Of course actual life in these foreign lands may be much different from the romantic versions depicted. However, for the purposes of coming up with with a stimulating roleplay scenario, embrace and exaggerate stereotypes and factual deficiencies if desired to heighten the appeal. You can even experience the thrill of "breaking" social taboos as you sample forbidden pleasures in your private, pretend play. Choose an exotic culture from modern or historic times and select a few erotic elements to weave into your scenario.

- You can pretend to be a visiting traveller enjoying special treatment
- Either one or both of you can play as a native citizen or foreigner
- Enhance your play with as many elements of the culture as you can find (fruit, clothing, music, etc.)
- Watch a movie or documentary about aspects of the culture that intrigue you

Sex With The Stars

Television, movie, music and sports stars seem to fascinate us for various reasons. You may even have dreams of being a star yourself and enjoying the glamorous life in the spotlight. Whether it's their talents, skills, money or fame, having sex with a celebrity is high on the list of most popular fantasies for both men and women. Choose a star to be the center of your roleplay scenario. The complimentary character can be an agent, promoter, servant, fan or even another star. Depending on the personalities involved and the type of fantasy that gets you aroused, come up with an appropriate setting (back stage, award ceremony, limousine, etc.) to play out your sexy encounter.

- Scan a few tabloids to find a fun scandal to inspire your roleplay ideas (they may be about celebrities other than your fantasy star)
- Feel free to mix and match celebrities in your roleplay with pretend affairs or marriage

Television Turn Ons

There is bound to be a television show that has grabbed your interest enough to watch at least a few episodes. Whether it's a comedy, drama, game show or even a "reality" program that appeals to you, various elements of the show could be borrowed for your erotic pleasure. There may even be a favourite show that you grew up with that featured in your fantasies or wet dreams. Television may have had a very powerful influence on your developing sexual awareness as a teenager even shaping some of your future desires. Choose a television show that you either watch today or fondly remember watching to base your roleplay scenario on. Use part of the story line in an episode or pretend to be the characters in your own erotic episode.

- Watch a few episodes of your show together to refresh your memory of the characters and their personalities
- Although implied and explicit sex is more common on television today, make up your own dirty variations for older, more family friendly shows
- Consider what the characters would do while not on camera if they were real (extend their lives beyond the show)
- When watching TV with your partner, keep an eye out for sexy scenes you can play out together in more explicit detail

Sexy Songs

Music has a powerful effect on our emotions. The music itself can be slow and intimate or fast paced and passionate just like sex. Words and phrases in the songs can also resonate with us in many different ways. Even the type of singing voice influences how we respond to the song. Intense memories can be associated with songs we've heard during certain events in our lives. When we hear the song, the memories come flooding back. Many couples even have their own special songs that bring back memories of their love together. Choose a song to inspire an erotic roleplay scenario. Use the title, style of music, elements of the story line or even certain phrases to base your idea on.

- Consider whether or not you want the song playing during your roleplay
- When just making love, spice up your sex life by playing different types of mood music
- Experiment pacing your sensual pleasuring activities to the tempo of the music

Strange Bedfellows

Sometimes the best sex can come when you are having fun being silly or when you get the naughty feeling you're doing something completely wrong. Out of the ordinary sexual experiences can form lasting and treasured memories so why not try to create as many as you can. Choose any two characters that you think would make the weirdest, strangest or most bizarre pair of sexual partners. Create a roleplay idea involving these two characters getting it on together. They can be regular or famous people from any time in history or characters from books, movies or television.

- Each of you come up with a pair of characters and an erotic scenario then agree on the weirdest combination to play out
- Try a variation matching up people you know and roleplay how they would hook up together

Movie Magic

Almost every movie has at least one love scene, intimate moment or erotic situation that can form the basis of a sexy roleplay idea. Some sexy scenes are explicit enough to be enacted as is while others are more subtle and left to your imagination to be interpreted as desired. However, there are many other movie elements like costumes, props or settings that can feature prominently in your fantasies. Choose a movie and identify the scene or other aspect that you find erotically interesting. Decide to either act out a special scene together or create a new story line to give your version of the movie an alternate climactic ending.

- Watch the movie together to refresh your memory and discuss the details you find erotic
- Obtain costumes or props to help bring the movie to life
- Remember to keep the critics out of your play time and have fun regardless of your acting expertise
- Write a brief script if desired or just improv
- Practice with a few undress rehearsals and then setup one or more video cameras to capture the action

Lusty Locations

When looking to spice up a relationship, many creative couples seek out adventurous or novel places to make love. There are certain locations that enable sensual love making while others demand quicker acts of passion. A bedroom is a comfortable place to make love but there are so many exciting and lusty locations to enjoy deliciously wicked sex. Whether spontaneous and urgent or planned for frisky fun, sex in new locations can be extremely thrilling. Choose a unique or exotic location that you think would be an amazing place to make out. Come up with a roleplay idea set in this location. You don't actually need to have sex in that location as long as you can pretend you're there using any props available to make it seem more real. Identify the elements of the location that you find arousing and then try to recreate them as much as possible if you're not actually able to have sex there (yet).

- Remember that for some locations, there are pleasurable sex activities other than intercourse
- Oral and manual stimulation can be just as satisfying and more practical in certain types of locations
- See our EzineArticle "69 Places For Passion - Lusty Locations to Make Love" online for more ideas

Steamy Stories

From suggestively randy romance novels to explicit erotica, there are thousands of books and short stories available to inspire your desire with love or lust. Creative writers have dreamed up highly imaginative settings and scenarios for their characters to enjoy each other. Their steamy stories come in all kinds of varieties to suit every interest. Choose an erotic book or sexy short story to inspire your roleplay idea. Enact a specific scene as written or use parts of the story to come up with your own scenario. Try using the story, chapter or book title as the basis for your idea or just scan it for a juicy part to play out. Romance novels tend to have captivating book covers which could also inspire your roleplay scenario - you don't even need to read the book.

- Try reading short erotic passages from various books to each other
- Scan a new book of short erotic stories, pick one just by it's title and use that story to inspire your roleplay scenario

More Sexy Ideas

We hope you're always on the look out for ways to enhance your relationship and spice up your love life. We believe a vibrant sex life is essential to maintaining a healthy and happy relationship. It's also a vital aspect of your personal well being. The shared intimacy and pleasures of lovemaking is something we all need. But we also crave passion and excitement to keep us feeling more alive. Satisfy your desires by continuing to learn about and experiment with creative ways to make sex wildly fun, exciting and thrilling together. Challenge each other to step out of your sexual comfort zone and explore your full erotic potential.

Come visit **www.frisky-sexual-fantasies.com** to discover more sexy fantasy and roleplay ideas for couples on our blog. We also run a number of other blogs and websites that you may find interesting:

- www.couplesgames.net
- www.friskyforeplay.com/ideas
- www.adultboardgamedesign.com
- www.sexquestionsforcouples.com
- www.sexysuggestions.com

You may also enjoy our other books available from Amazon:

- 469 Fun Sex Questions for Couples
- Sex Games & Foreplay Ideas for Couples

If you have an iPhone or iPad, check out our two creative sex apps currently available in iTunes. Just do a search for:

- iLoveRandomSex
- Succulent Expressions

List of Sexy Scenarios

Here is a list of all the frisky sexual fantasies and erotic roleplay ideas with page numbers so that you can select one based on just it's title.

Stranger Attraction

Wild Westerns

Tantalizing Times

Fairy Tale Fantasies

Wanton Witches & Wizards

Made in the USA
Las Vegas, NV
29 November 2024